"Stepping beyond the powerless platitudes of religion into the process of radical transformation, Randall Worley offers us the journey of a lifetime—from wandering to wonder, from striving to rest. Deeply felt and transparent. This is the stuff we need to hear. If you feel like the winds of life too often work against you rather than for you, read this book and reset your sails. Freedom and peace await."

—*Ted Dekker*
New York Times bestselling author

"There are many books collecting dust in my library about how to 'discover your purpose,' but comparatively few that teach—from insight and experience—the process needed to truly live from this wellspring of purpose once we've discovered it. In these pages, you'll discover Randall Worley, a seasoned guide in navigating life's path from discovery to obedience to mystery; from staying in those grueling transitions and letting go into rest. If you're looking for quick-fixes and platitudes, look somewhere else. But if you're looking for a trustworthy field manual for manifesting what makes you come most alive, *Wandering and Wondering: The Process That Activates Your Purpose* is for you."

—*Mike Morrell*
MikeMorrell.org
Coauthor with Richard Rohr,
The Divine Dance: The Trinity and your Transformation

"Randall Worley's *Wandering and Wondering* is wisdom litera-
ture for our time. Weaving together psychological depth, spiritual
insight, pastoral sensitivity, and dirt-under-your-fingernails truth,
Randall takes you on a transformational journey. In a world full
of so much information, this is not a book that informs but one
that invites—an invitation to a different way of being in the world,
a deeper way of listening to God and to our own lives. Randall's
fatherly, incarnational wisdom profoundly shaped my own journey. I know it will shape yours."

—Jonathan Martin
Author, *How to Survive a Shipwreck* and *Prototype*
Pastor, Renovatus, Charlotte, NC

"*Wandering and Wondering* inspired me to trust and forced me to
react. It was like reading a beautiful invitation to rest while hearing a battle cry for transformation. I know this book will help you
navigate the beautiful tension of change and transition. It did it for
me! I can't wait to see your future after you access the revelation in
these hope-filled pages."

—Carlos A. Rodríguez
Chief Editor, HappySonship.com
Author, *Drop the Stones*

"I have a world of admiration for Randall Worley. Over the years
I've often found his words to be timely, and while the contents of
this book could speak volumes to any generation, I find its message
to be especially pertinent today. In *Wandering and Wondering*,
Randall guides us through the agony and adventure of true living
that only happens in the space between spaces and challenges us to
face uncertainty with hope and expectation!"

—John Mark McMillan
Christian singer/songwriter

"Have you wondered why things are going wrong in your life and you feel stuck? Have you ever wandered in dark places, unable to comprehend why your purpose still seems so distant? Well, then this book has arrived in your hands at a most serendipitous moment. In the introduction to *Wandering and Wondering*, Randall Worley challenges the prevailing success narrative of the day. In a culturally relevant way, he describes the false narrative in this way: 'Life…is not as simple as pointing the cursor of intention, clicking, and instantly having megabytes of clarity and direction at your disposal.' In the pages that follow, Randall presents you with the insights and encouragement you need to assist you in navigating through the space that exists between the *here* and *there*. Once you have read this book and you have been changed by it—and you will—then encourage your friends to get the book. You will be doing them a huge favor. I've been a close friend of Randall's for many years. I know of the skirmishes he has endured on the battlefields of life. I can say unequivocally that his personal life reflects the depth of his message, as you will see when he tells you his own story."

—Don Milam
Author, *The Ancient Language of Eden*

WANDERING
·AND·
WONDERING

RANDALL WORLEY

WANDERING
·AND·
WONDERING

WHITAKER
HOUSE

WANDERING AND WONDERING:
The Process That Brings Purpose

RandallWorley.com

ISBN: 978-1-62911-906-9
eBook ISBN: 978-1-62911-907-6
Printed in the United States of America
© 2017 Randall Worley

Whitaker House
1030 Hunt Valley Circle
New Kensington, PA 15068
www.whitakerhouse.com

Library of Congress Cataloging-in-Publication Data (Pending)

1 2 3 4 5 6 7 8 9 10 11 12 Ⱳ 25 24 23 22 21 20 19 18 17

CONTENTS

INTRODUCTION:
FRATERNAL TWINS OF DESTINY

Purpose has been a hot topic for several years, capturing the attention of those adrift in a culture of apathy and aimlessness. The burning desire to know why we are here is widespread, testifying to the fact that while we may know when we were born and to whom we were born, we still may not know *why* we were born.

Some people seem to know early on who they are and what they are here to do, while others wander through life wondering. A quote attributed to Mark Twain sums this up well: "The two most important days in your life are the day you were born, and the day you find out why." What happens in between those two great days of birth and discovery can certainly be perplexing. *Purpose*, which answers the question of *why*, can be realized in moment. *Process*, however, which seeks the answer of *how*, cannot be actualized as quickly. In other words, "an overnight success takes years."

Since I will be talking about process throughout this book, we should start with a basic definition: "Process is a systematic series of actions directed to some end: a continuous action…or series of changes taking place in a definite manner…the action of going forward or on."

That all sounds simple enough doesn't it? Or is it? The operative terms in the definition are *action*, *series of changes*, and *going forward*. Clearly, process is not a simple hop, skip, and jump away.

I don't want to sound like a cynic, but the popular culture has conditioned us to believe that everything, including destiny, is immediately "downloadable." Life, however, is not as simple as pointing the cursor of intention, clicking, and instantly having megabytes of clarity and direction at your disposal. *Between the realization and actualization of our purpose there is an evolving*—a long obedience in the same direction involving mystery, uncertainty, trusting, transitions, waiting, and doubting.

Purpose is certainly a far more palatable subject in today's culture of self-improvement than process because it seems to offer a free carpet ride from here to there without the hard work of transformation. In some ways this resembles the bait-and-switch tactics we see in the world of advertising. The fundamental approach of the advertising industry is to create a sense of need and urgency, or even scarcity—"limited time offer!" or "act now!" You are enticed by a bargain only to discover that what you want will cost far more than what was first proclaimed. "Buy now, pay later" has become the mantra, depriving of us of the skill of delayed gratification and resulting in compromising what we want most for what we can get now. In contrast, the dream of your destiny is free and comes as effortlessly as dreaming, but the journey toward actualizing your destiny is going to come with a cost.

I agree that purpose is vital to life. Dying is not life's greatest tragedy. The real tragedy is dying having never fully lived. Or to have lived your entire life fulfilling someone else's dream—your parents or some other significant influencer—instead of cultivating the purpose that only your uniquely designed one-of-a-kind-ness can accomplish.

However, it is my intention in this book to show that *purpose* cannot be fully realized if its fraternal twin *process* is not recognized. They may not resemble each other, they may not be identical twins, but they have an inseparable bond because they were formed together in the womb of destiny.

The moment we receive the revelation of our purpose is similar to the ecstatic feeling a woman has upon discovering that she is pregnant for the very first time. When your "pregnancy test" of purpose comes back positive, you are brimming with excitement and glowing with anticipation. But the initial euphoria of conception is quickly followed by the inevitable: nausea, appetite changes, erratic mood swings, and a changing center of gravity as new life is formed inside of you. You will be stretched in more ways than one! You will wonder, *Am I really ready for this? Do I have the aptitude and competency to carry what I've conceived and to deliver?*

Purpose and process are not in conflict, nor do they contradict one another, although it often may seem that way. The real truth of life's journey is that it has always been held in a tension of contradictions, conflict, and confusion. All of life exists in tension. The polarity between purpose and process can be paralyzing at times. But just like you can't experience love without fear, faith without doubt, peace without frustration, light without darkness, life without death, success without failure, you can't experience purpose without process. So let's explore this tension and discover the path that leads to our destiny.

1

WEAVING A TAPESTRY

Our lives are truly a tapestry of pleasure and pain, beauty and ugliness, woven over time. Thousands of thin and variegated strands stretched taut across the weaver's loom are intricately intertwined to create the tapestry of rugs that hang on walls or adorn our floors. The underside of a tapestry appears tangled, knotted, and frayed, but it does not reveal the pattern of the upper side, only the process. The vivid patterns with rich hues are the artistic craft of a weaver who works on the underside so that the top is a beautiful picture. This process is a picture of how truth is woven into the very fabric of our lives. God sends and spins strands of singular truths over time. Sometimes the threads are brightly colored or pleasant pastels and other times they are dark and difficult to understand.

I suppose the most-quoted Scripture when it comes to experiencing the unexplainable is *"All things work together for good, for those who are called according to his purpose"* (Romans 8:28). I am sure you know the feeling of hanging by a single thread of truth, trying desperately to make sense of what you are going through. It really is more about the broader context of what God is weaving in you than what is worrying you at any given moment. If we fixate on an isolated portion of the overall pattern in our purpose, we can't see the beauty of the whole tapestry.

One of the names of God in Scripture is *Jehovah-Rophe*, which means "the Lord, our Healer." I read many years ago a Jewish legend that the pronunciation of this name sounds like the whisper made by the weaver's shuttle as it moves back and forth across the loom, drawing in and integrating each thread into the whole of the tapestry. Our bodies, like the thousands of threads in a tapestry, are woven together by miles of veins and neuropathways. Healing may happen at a physical level in an instant yet the recipient still remains ill at the emotional or spiritual level. You can experience healing in your body and not be made whole because your memories are still pulsating with pain.

God is interested in the whole tapestry. He desires to deal with more than the symptoms. His work systemically deals with the spirit, soul, and body. Pathology and psychology may bring health to the body and soul but only soteriology, the complete work of salvation, brings complete wholeness. Salvation takes the loose and frayed ends of our emotions and wraps them in threads of truth, giving symmetry and sense to our lives. You are not what you were, and you are not what you will be. The shuttle is still moving rhythmically, back and forth, in the deepest part of who you are, weaving His ultimate purpose. Rest in the resonance of *Jehovah-Rophe's* full restoration.

My Process

My journey of over five decades on this earth has taught me that *our process is in direct proportion to our purpose.* The greater the purpose in one's life, usually the more protracted the process is.

This is borne out in the sagas of both historical and contemporary sojourners.

Allow me to provide some context before diving into my life process that led me to finding purpose. To begin with, I realize that we should never allow our past to hold our future hostage. Your past is in the past, and your history has been swallowed up by *His*-story. As a believer, I received a new identity the moment I accepted God's version of me. *"This means that anyone who belongs to Christ has become a new person. The old life is gone; a new life has begun!"* (2 Corinthians 5:17 NLT). But in one of his last letters, the apostle Paul wrote,

> *I don't mean to say I am perfect. I haven't learned all I should even yet, but I keep working toward that day when I will finally be all that Christ saved me for and wants me to be. No, dear brothers, I am still not all I should be, but I am bringing all my energies to bear on this one thing: Forgetting the past and looking forward to what lies ahead, I strain to reach the end of the race and receive the prize for which God is calling us up to heaven because of what Christ Jesus did for us.*
>
> (Philippians 3:12–14 TLB)

I think Paul was making it clear that we all struggle with forgetting what we should remember, and remembering what we should forget. His past included radical acts of terrorism, utter hubris, and self-righteousness. But even the shameful, egregious parts of his past would better equip him to receive the marvelous revelation of God's grace and unconditional love at work in the warp and woof of his life.

Isaiah said that God *"blots out"* (Isaiah 43:25)—forgets—our sins. But, if God knows all things, how can He not remember our past? Maybe, when He remembers, He remembers it differently than we do. We cannot wrap our minds around it, but God has the ability to see where you've been, who you are at this moment, and where you will be and who you will become, all at the same time. That ability is His *providence*—literally, to "see beforehand." Our vision of our life is peripherally limited compared to His. Providence is God's instant panoramic perspective of our past, present, and future. *"And we know that all that happens to us is working for our good if we love God and are fitting into his plans"* (Romans 8:28 TLB).

The story that follows has not defined me but has sometimes confined me, as well as become integral to my process. I start with my father and mother, knowing today, but not in my earlier years, that even though I came into this earthly existence *through* them, I did not come *from* them. I didn't chose them as parents and they didn't chose me either. Rather, "[God] *chose us in him before the foundation of the world"* (Ephesians 1:4). We are not merely the product of our parents' passion. With all due respect to our mothers, their wombs were merely a dressing room for us to manifest out of eternity and into time. But as with all child-parent relationships, much of what I became was due to their influence and imprinting.

We are not merely the product of our parents' passion. With all due respect to our mothers, their wombs were merely a dressing room for us to manifest out of eternity and into time.

As Brené Brown says,

Our lives are a collection of stories, the truth about who we are, what we believe, what we came from, how we struggled and how we are strong. When we let go of what people think, and own our story we gain access to our worthiness, the feeling that we are enough just as we are, and that we are worthy of love and belonging. Owning our story can be hard but not nearly as difficult as spending our lives running from it. Embracing our vulnerabilities is risky but not nearly as dangerous as giving up on love and belonging and joy—the experiences that make us the most vulnerable. Only when we are brave enough to explore the darkness will we discover the infinite power of our light.[1]

My father was born in 1928, a child of the Great Depression. He grew up in poverty in southern Appalachia. The remote mountain-culture economy included logging, farming, and, as you might suspect, corncob pipe-smoking moonshiners.

Along with his parents and six siblings, he lived in a one-room, primitive log cabin perched on the side of a mountain. He described his childhood home as having no windows, cracks in the floor wide enough to see the chickens scratching on the ground beneath, and gaps in the wall big enough that winter snows would cover their quilts in the morning. Water for drinking, cooking, and bathing had to be collected from a nearby spring and carried several hundred yards back to the cabin. Following in his father's footsteps, his first job at age of twelve was pulling a crosscut saw as a hardened lumberjack cursed him, spit tobacco juice, and told him not to "ride the saw." In other words, "You better pull your weight, boy!"

Many times during the harsh winters, my father would come home from the logging camps with his clothes frozen. He quickly went from a boy to a man by scraping out a living through much hardship. I later found out something intriguing about the Worley name while on an ancestry website. "Worley" is a derivation of an English surname *Warley*, meaning "wood clearing." Coincidence? Maybe.

At fifteen or so, my father moved with his family to south-central North Carolina to work in the textile mill boom of the 1940s. Due to his brutal upbringing, my father had numerous encounters with the police during this period. By no means

---

1. Brené Brown, *The Hustle for Worthiness* (DVD).

do I want to sound like I am vilifying my father. He, like so many others of his era, was a product of his unfortunate environment. His life resembled what Johnny Cash describes in his song "A Boy Named Sue": "I grew up fast and I grew up mean. My fist got hard and my wits got keen." In one of his barroom skirmishes, Dad so badly injured a man that the man was admitted to intensive care, landing my dad in jail. Years later, when Dad would retell these surreal stories about his early life, I realized that it was nothing short of a miracle that he wasn't killed or incarcerated for life.

After jumping bail from an arrest, he lied about his age, joined the army, and was sent to Japan in the aftermath of World War II, where he was stationed for almost three years. He met my mother after serving in the military and they started their family with not much more than what he had growing up. Not long after that, my father became a believer, due my mom's faithful witness, and subsequently became a minister. His transformation from renegade to reverend set my vocation in motion years before I was ever born.

Their first child, my only sister, was born premature and died within hours. Their second child, my only living sibling, was born physically disfigured with a harelip and cleft palate, and later was diagnosed with a mental disability. Their third child was another boy who died at ten months from acute pneumonia. I was their last child. Just after my birth, my mother developed tumors in her ovaries requiring surgery that rendered her unable to have any more children. The trail of the repeated tragedies they suffered through the death of children and living just above the poverty line was difficult for them to process.

My father never showed favoritism to me over my developmentally-challenged brother, but he began to tell me from an early age that God had told him that He would give him another son who would do great things. I remember in grade school having a love for reading, and, in time, I began to realize that I was becoming, in essence, the last-born first born. My brother's inability to read and write created a role reversal that I struggled to understand. Of all their offspring, why was I the child who survived and received this privilege? Why was I one of the two surviving children to receive such a promise for what I would do in life?

Dad routinely reminded me of the providential nature of my birth and that I was smart. You would think that hearing this throughout my developmental years would have had a profoundly positive effect on me; however, it was just the opposite. I struggled with many insecurities and intense feelings of inadequacy. I couldn't process my dad's praise of what I was destined to become. I wrongfully assumed that due to his many struggles, he was seeking to live vicariously through me. I was convinced that I was, at best, an average child, and no amount of affirmation was able to convince me otherwise. I adopted the philosophy that "I would rather have an inferiority complex and be pleasantly surprised, than have a superiority complex and be rudely awakened."[2]

We are not who we think we are, and we are not who others *think we are—yet we think this must be who we are.*

It was not until I was in my fifties that I began to believe that my dad may have been right all along. I slowly began to recognize that my father's struggle and my own struggle had been integral parts of my process. We are not who we think we are, and we are not who others think we are—yet we think this must be who we are.

> Every one of us is shadowed by an illusory person: a false self. This is the man [or woman] that I want myself to be but who cannot exist, because God does not know anything about him [or her].[3]

---

2. Quote attributed to American writer, actress, and inventor Vanna Bonta.
3. Thomas Merton, quoted in Fr. Richard Rohr, "The Illusion of an Autonomous Self," Center for Action and Contemplation, https://cac.org/illusion-autonomous-self-2016-08-03/ (accessed February 8, 2017).

The words of Marianne Williamson have resonated with me so many times over the years as I have struggled with questions about the process leading to my purpose:

> Our deepest fear is not that we are inadequate. Our deepest fear is that we are powerful beyond measure. It is our light, not our darkness, that most frightens us. We ask ourselves, Who am I to be brilliant, gorgeous, talented, fabulous? Actually, who are you not to be?[4]

My insatiable appetite for reading at an early age, which could have been due to my attempts to compensate for my perceived lack of intelligence, diminished as I grew into my teen years. After making it through high school by the skin of my teeth, my father convinced me to enroll in college. Still, I had this underlying notion that I was doing what my father wanted me to do—not what *I* wanted to do. Reluctantly, I started my first year surrounded by students who seemed to know exactly what they wanted to do in life. Just like in high school, I barely passed my freshman year. Harboring feelings of ineptness, I returned my sophomore year with a new determination to apply myself. That first semester, I went from being on academic probation to being on the dean's list. I was as surprised as everybody else. That's when I began to discover that the lessons I would learn in life would not be learned in a course but on a course.

After finishing my undergraduate studies, I enrolled in graduate school motivated by the need to *prove* myself rather than to *improve* myself. Did I believe almost forty years ago that I would be a public speaker or even an author? No! A thousand times no! I didn't believe that I was enough. The voice of my inner critic, not Satan the accuser, but the voice I hear the most—*my voice*—had conditioned me to believe that I would never be enough. We are ashamed of our weakness but God is actually attracted to them.

---

4. Marianne Williamson, *A Return to Love: Reflections on the Principles of "A Course in Miracles"* (New York: Harper Collins, 1993), 190.

He simply can't resist our feeble frame. "The most successful people are not perfect, but the imperfect who dare to believe that they can despite the damning verdict."[5]

We are ashamed of our weakness but God is actually attracted to them. He simply can't resist our feeble frame.

Process in the Bible

Everyone and everything God has ever used, even the inanimate, goes through a process. There are absolutely no exceptions, as far as I can tell—even though human nature is to go around rather than through.

There are many examples that illustrate this principle. My references will include contemporary best-selling authors' insights on process as well as the ancient text of Scripture, which demonstrates the power of process perhaps more than any other text. René Girard wrote that the Bible is "a text in travail,"[6] suggesting that even in the narrative of Scripture, what man says about God and life in it was, and is, evolving in a process.

Have you ever wondered why, after the ruinous fall of the first man and woman, God didn't restore and redeem everything back to its original state of perfection within their lifetimes? It would seem that the Creator could have just reset everything back to its original glorious and perfect state. Why was it necessary for thousands of years and generations to pass until even now, in the twenty-first century, we are still looking back, trying to make sense of it all? What we know now is more than those men who were

5. Bangambiki Habyarimana, *Pearls of Eternity*, quoted on Goodreads, https://www.goodreads.com/work/quotes/52362912-pearls-of-eternity (accessed February 17, 2017).
6. Walter Burkert, René Girard, Jonathan Z. Smith, *Violent Origins* (Stanford, CA: Stanford University Press, 1987), 141.

writing the Scriptures, and what will be known is a reflection of the ever-evolving consciousness of humans in process.

Here are just a few examples from Scripture to posture your thinking for the chapters that follow. In the famous story of David conquering Goliath, even the stones he used played an important role. The five smooth stones that David retrieved from a brook as ammunition to slay the giant had been smoothed in a process over hundreds of years, waiting for the day when David would answer the challenge. Being a marksman, David knew the stones had to be smooth to maintain trajectory when released from his crude leather sling. As he deposited the river stones in his shepherd's bag, I'm not sure David realized that these stones were a symbol of how God would take him through a similar process in the years to come.

How did the stones become so smooth? Over time, the once-rough stones tumbled along the bottom of the brook, wearing off their jagged edges. During floods, the rushing current violently bounced them along the bed of the brook. In times of drought, when the brook diminished to a trickle, the stones were exposed to bake in the sun. In his hand, David held a token—the tacit truth of God's process that eventually finds its purpose.

Joseph, a dreamer extraordinaire at just seventeen, would awaken from a dream of such epic proportion that it would shape the destiny of his immediate family and an entire nation. He was clueless that one night of deep REM sleep would take him on a thirteen-year roller coaster ride, beginning with the visceral jealousy of his brothers stripping him of his coat of many colors. After his brothers conspired to murder him, threw him into a pit, and sold him into slavery, Joseph was falsely accused of raping the wife of his employer and was sentenced to imprisonment in a dungeon cell. His cellmates were released and soon forgot his interpretation of their dreams that got them sprung. After years of being the target of jealousy, rejection, false accusation, and betrayal, the dream he had was finally realized. At longs last, Joseph sat on the throne as the prince of Egypt.

The psalmist explained the alchemy of Joseph's process in this way: "...*Joseph, who was sold as a slave. His feet were hurt with fetters; his neck was put in a collar of iron; until what he had said came to pass, the word* [the dream] *of the* LORD *tested him*" (Psalm 105:17–19). I'm sure with every movement, the rattling of his chains is a dank prison cell must have caused him to think, *Why did I have that dream?* and *Why has all this happened to me?* and *How could such a vivid dream turn into a nightmare of contradiction?*

This verse made sense to me years ago when I was going through what seemed to be an endless night of injustices—certainly not to the extent of Joseph but still intense for me.

All storms, and I do mean all of them,

eventually run out of rain.

I came home from my office one day mentally and emotionally spent, running on fumes. As a young man with many demands on my life at the time, coupled with repeated inequities, I was in a period of questioning my dream of becoming a visionary leader and communicator. My closest colleagues had mounted a conspiracy campaign against me with the intention of removing me from my position. Like Joseph's brothers, they had contempt for me, a young dreamer. I had experienced God's favor in my life, but things were now less than favorable. My dream seemed like a nightmare and I was in the starring role. I didn't know at the time that all storms, and I do mean all of them, eventually run out of rain.

When I walked in the door that evening, my wife was standing in the kitchen cooking beef liver in an iron skillet. She knew I liked this particular dish but she seldom ever cooked it because she detested both the sight and taste of it. Knowing her aversion for liver, I asked her why she was cooking it. She had been struggling with anemia for some time, constantly challenged with little to no stamina. The supplements her physician had prescribed had not improved her condition at all. She told me that earlier that day, he had told her to purchase the liver, a rich source of iron, and to cook it in a black cast-iron skillet. He explained that the liver would be infused with iron from the hot skillet. His theory was that ingesting liver that had been infused with iron could be the home remedy to her anemia. The connection between Joseph's ordeal and my wife cooking liver may sound odd but I instantly understood that all of those intense years of Joseph being fettered in iron manacles had not weakened him but instead had infused him with the strength he would need to endure experiencing an "overnight success," the moment when he would go from the prison to the palace. Like Joseph, I didn't need to jump from the frying pan into the fire. My crisis was cooking and the iron of fortitude was penetrating my persona.

Every biblical character was taken through a process, without exception. Just the mention of Moses' name, for example, summons images of a man larger than life. But that larger-than-life image we have of him standing on a rock, overlooking the Red Sea, and parting the waters would come eighty years after Pharaoh's daughter plucked him from the Nile, sparing him from being the victim of filicide.

Moses was groomed in Pharaoh's palace for forty years, only to commit aggravated murder and spend forty years as a fugitive herding sheep in a desert for his father-in-law, which must have seemed a complete contradiction to the dreams that had always been in his heart. The primeval occupation of a shepherd was considered menial work. Shepherds were culturally ostracized and were not even allowed to testify in court. Moses was marginalized, reduced to solitary work in the wilderness when he thought he was supposed to be a savior. An emancipator relegated to an employee.

Then God began to speak to him from, of all things, a burning bush. Certainly Moses had seen a bush spontaneously combust during his many years in the blistering desert. What was different about this one that captivated his attention? This one, although ablaze, was not turning to ashes. Intrigued by this phenomenon, he approached to get a closer look. Maybe God spoke to Moses through this medium because his original burning passion to be the deliverer of his people was now only a dying ember. The voice that called him by name required him to remove his shoes before the conversation continued. To this day in certain Asian cultures, there a custom of removing one's shoes before stepping over the threshold of a home. Moses was definitely at a threshold moment in his life. Moses spent forty years on a job that had nothing to do with his destiny. Was Moses a failure during those forty years of his life? Absolutely not! God was showing him that what he had "walked through" and "stepped in" during those years of wondering about how his life had turned out needed to be removed. At eighty years of age, with a criminal record and possibly feeling forgotten, the voice of God speaks to him from, of all places, a burning bush. He had been raised in the lavish palace of Pharaoh and educated in Egypt, but his practicum was in a desolate desert.

Process in Our Lives

Like I said, the real lessons of life are not learned in a course but on a course. Our teachers aren't just found in classrooms but in crisis and relational conflict.

> Consider it a sheer gift, friends, when tests and challenges come at you from all sides. You know that under pressure, your faith-life is forced into the open and shows its true colors. So don't try to get out of anything prematurely. Let it do its work so you become mature and well-developed, not deficient in any way. (James 1:2 MSG)

Pause for a moment and take a look around the room. Everything from your clothes to the chair you're sitting on, the walls, the doors, and the book (or e-reader) you are holding in your hand came from raw materials that had to go through a process before being useful. A seed fell onto the ground and in the darkness of the soil it broke open, putting down roots, struggling to break through the soil toward the sun. Seasons of drought and deluge came and went before the trees were mature enough to be harvested and milled into the paper on which my words are written.

It may sound incredible for me to say that the greatest struggle of your life is behind you, compared to the one you may be in now. You don't remember it, but your greatest struggle in life is not what you've been through to date but the throes of childbirth. You've never heard of a baby being born laughing have you? No, we all emerged into this world gasping for breath and spend the rest of our lives having the breath knocked out of you by circumstances, moments of astonishment, and trying to keep the pace.

In the chapters that follow, I will share with you my ongoing curriculum: failing successfully, the benefit of doubt, what happens while you wait, navigating transitions, and connecting the dots.

In the continuum of life between birth and burial there are many twists and turns. You've probably heard the often-used analogy of the dash on a tombstone between the date of birth and the date of death. What matters more than the dates, the story goes, is what happens in the dash—the time in between. The dash, though minuscule, symbolizes an entire life. Process is what happens in this vaporous in-between. What you will go through on your journey—the successes and failures, the wins and losses, the joys and the sorrows—are commensurate to what you are going through because what we focus on always determines what we miss.

There is no tombstone in Israel bearing the name of the greatest emancipator of history, Jesus of Nazareth, indicating he lived only thirty-three years. In fact, He lived all but three years of His life in almost complete anonymity. Jesus, God in flesh, didn't just appear on the planet as a fully-formed superhuman. No, the infinite One was subjected in every way to the process of becoming human— being born, crawling, learning to walk and talk, maturing, learning and earning, experiencing the full range of human emotions. The writer of Hebrews said, *"Though he was God's Son, he learned trusting-obedience by what he suffered, just as we do"* (Hebrew 5:8 MSG). Jesus referred to Himself as the "Son of Man" far more than the "Son of God," to emphasize His humanness. The recognition that the boy Jesus (see Luke 2) was a prodigy in no way gave Him an exemption. If anyone had a right to a sense of entitlement, He did. But you will not find even a hint of it in His developmental years or in His teaching. Jesus lived obediently with His simple parents, maturing, growing up in body, mind, and spirit. One thing is for certain: the brevity of His life by comparison in no way diminishes the gravity of His life. When considering mortality rates, it seems He finished early, but He did finish well because of the process.

> But even before I was born, God **chose** me and **called** me by
> his marvelous grace. (Galatians 1:15 NLT)

Your purpose and process were chosen by God long before you were born. The greatest challenge of your life is to hear His call, live out His call, and finish well. That is the goal. To one day realize, as Paul did, that *"I have fought the good fight, I have finished the race, I have kept the faith"* (2 Timothy 4:7).

But you will only be able to finish the race well if you are living inside the tension of purpose and process, as Christ Himself did.

Wonderings

Exercises to Do While Wandering

Write down ten events in your life (good or bad) that have shaped you, helped make you who you are today, or landed you where you are today. They can be major events like an adoption, a death, or a vacation; or they can be insignificant things that left a great impression, such as the words of a coach or teacher, harsh taunts from a bully, or a single statement from a parent.

1. _____

_____

_____

2. _____

_____

_____

3. _____

_____

_____

4. _____

_____

_____

5. _____

_____

_____

6. _____

_____

_____

7. _____

_____

_____

8. _____

_____

_____

9. _____

_____

_____

10. _____

_____

_____

Reflect on God's hand and timing in these events.

REFLECTIONS

_____
_____
_____
_____
_____
_____
_____
_____
_____
_____
_____
_____
_____
_____
_____
_____
_____
_____
_____

2

AN OVERNIGHT SUCCESS TAKES YEARS

Last chapter I stated that an overnight success takes years. It sounds like a bit of a paradox or oxymoron doesn't it? Sort of like "open secret," "act naturally," or "deafening silence." We hear the rags-to-riches stories all the time. But an *overnight success* is when a person, previously unheard of, suddenly, like a meteor, has their face plastered everywhere—TV, magazines, the Internet—and they, or their business, instantly become a household name. One day a struggling unknown, the next a trending celebrity or Fortune-500 phenomenon.

A Forty-Year Overnight Success Story

But how long does it *really* take to create an overnight success? It took Fred Smith eleven years from the time his idea was conceived to the moment he delivered his first overnight package. Fred Smith is founder, president, and CEO of FedEx. The familiar advertising slogan "When it absolutely positively has to be there overnight" caught America's attention in 1978 and seemed, at the time, ridiculously ambitious. In those days, the time between sending and receiving any package of goods moved at a snail's pace.

Back in 1962, Fred had written a paper for his college economics class on the concept of overnight delivery service. He received a C on the paper and his professor said, "The concept is interesting and well-formed, but in order to earn better than a C grade, the idea must be feasible."

The idea incubated for years and, shortly after college, Fred was sent to Vietnam as a Marine, where he studied the Air Force's logistics systems. When he returned to the states in 1970, he bought an aircraft maintenance company, Ark Aviation Sales, and started trading in used jets.

By 1973, he had copied the military's logistics operation with a small fleet of fourteen Falcon 20 jets, and, eleven years after his professor's repudiation, he shipped his first parcel.

Fred successfully raised twenty-nine million dollars in venture capital funds to get the business off the ground, but lost all of it within the first two years of business. Desperation quickly set in, so with his last five thousand dollars, Fred flew to Las Vegas and bet all his remaining money on a game of blackjack. He won twenty-seven thousand dollars, which paid the fuel bill due and kept FedEx in business.

Roger Frock, his business partner, remembers the Monday after:

> I asked Fred where the funds had come from, and he responded, "The meeting with the General Dynamics board was a bust and I knew we needed money for Monday, so I took a plane to Las Vegas and won $27,000." I said, "You mean you took our last $5,000—how could you do that?" He shrugged his shoulders and said, "What difference does it make? Without the funds for the fuel we couldn't have flown anyway."[7]

---

7. Roger Frock, *Changing How the World Does Business: FedEx's Incredible Journey to Success* (San Francisco: Berrett-Koehler Publishers, Inc., 2006), 101.

FedEx experienced one financial crisis after another, but Fred managed to *survive* and even *thrive* through two recessions—the collapse of the dotcom bubble in the late 1990s and the Global Financial Crisis in 2008. Now, fifty years after that college term paper, Fred has built a two-billion-dollar fortune as CEO of a company that ships over a billion packages a year.

From overnight successes to overnight deliveries, everything must take longer before it can happen faster.

Most "overnight" successes actually take years. There are occasional anomalies, but they are exceptions, not the norm. The list of so-called "zero to heroes" is exhaustive; many of the entrepreneurs, innovators, musicians, and world-class athletes that are household names now, were once homeless, unemployed, rejected, struggling nobodies. Before enjoying celebrity status, they endured the crucible of *process* that separated the inferior alloy of their egos from the gift they are now known for.

From overnight successes to overnight deliveries,
everything must take longer before it can happen faster.

For example, let's say an unknown author becomes a *New York Times* best-seller. Even if it was his or her first novel, chances are great that the novel took months or even years to write, and it was certainly not written overnight. My friend and best-selling author Ted Dekker told me that he wrote almost one million words before being published, and even after getting his first publishing deal, he doubted whether anyone would want to buy his book. Since that time he has sold ten million copies of his books. Or again, over 140 publishers rejected Jack Canfield, author of the much-acclaimed *Chicken Soup for the Soul*. Now it has been translated into forty-three languages worldwide and sold over five hundred million copies.

Development in the Darkness

Overnight? More likely months or years full of long, dark nights. That can sound gloomy, but let me explain further the process we are in and what is developing. It's a bit like old-fashioned photography. Today, taking a picture is as easy as pointing your digital device and clicking—instantly you have it. But in its early days, photography was a process. A camera was aimed at a scene or subject. Then, once focus was acquired by dialing the lens aperture, the shutter was triggered, allowing enough light into the lens to burn a negative of the image onto a celluloid film. That negative remained in the housing of the camera until it was taken to a darkroom for development, where the negatives were projected onto paper that was then dipped, or "processed," into a series of chemical baths. If the paper came out of the chemicals too soon or too late, it was either under- or overexposed. Expose the negative to light before it was processed and the image would be ruined forever. But leave it in the dark room for the right amount of time, and it came out perfect.

Maybe God works the same way. The aura around God is usually portrayed as light. However, our first introduction to God's creative work begins with darkness and chaos. *"First this: God created the Heavens and the Earth—all you see, all you don't see. Earth was a soup of nothingness"* (Genesis 1:1 MSG). John emphatically said, *"God is light, and in him is no darkness at all"* (1 John 1:5). But David wrote, *"He made darkness his secret place; his pavilion round about him were dark waters and thick clouds of the skies"* (Psalm 18:11 KJV). Are the psalmist and the apostle contradicting one another? Is this a mistake in Scripture? David clears it up for us in Psalm 139:11–12: *"If I say, 'Surely the darkness shall cover me, and the light about me be night,' even the darkness is not dark to you; the night is bright as the day; for darkness is as light with you."*

Perception really is everything, isn't it?

If the doors of perception were cleansed everything would appear to man as it is, infinite. For man has closed himself up, till he sees all things thro' narrow chinks of his cavern.[8]

The Jewish perspective of achievement is seen in the way in which they chart the Jewish year. The Gregorian calendar, the internationally accepted way of measuring time, follows the sun, an ever-present source of light. The Jewish calendar, conversely, follows the moon, the natural satellite of the night that continuously waxes and wanes. When the moon is full, even the darkest night has a degree of illumination. But for half of the month, the light wanes until it disappears completely, when the only way forward is through focus and tireless commitment.

Just so, real success occurs on a long and winding road that must be illuminated by determination and perseverance. As King Solomon wrote, "*The righteous falls seven times, and rises again*" (Proverbs 24:16). Solomon was not born wise; he grew that way. He was not great *in spite* of his falling; he was great *because* of his falling. Or as Robert G. Allen says, "There is no failure. Only feedback."

Expediting Process at the Expense of Experience

Today, however, our culture reflects a growing impatience with the process of life. We have amazing technology that grants us instant access to whatever we need with the simple click of a cursor. The advent of the search engine has enabled us to cut to the chase when it comes to finding the un-findable. What was at one time a painstaking process of locating vital information by sifting through reams of the written word has been bypassed with a click. By simply entering a keyword, you gain access to everything you wanted to know that has been amassed and downloaded on the worldwide web.

---

8. William Blake, *The Marriage of Heaven and Hell*, plate 14.

There are apps for everything—from games to escape boredom to navigation assistance that routes us to our desired destination. It has been said that in today's culture TGIF is not just an acronym for a chain of restaurants, neither does it mean Thank God It's Friday, but it refers to our addiction to Twitter, Google, iPhone, and Facebook. It is not my intention to sound critical—I too find myself tethered to my smart phone, incessantly checking emails, texts, social media, or googling what I want to know. I, too, can't imagine going offline or unplugging. I've fallen prey to "FOMO"—Fear of Missing Out! But if we are totally dependent on software, we will bypass learning to carry out tasks that we don't understand. We will never acquire the new skills that come from mastering a task, or the horizons that those skills open up. "We have allowed technology to beat our imaginations into submission and have become tourist rather than travelers."[9]

Once upon a time, when you didn't know how to do something, you had to either find someone who knew how to do it, find a book about it, or, God forbid, figure it out yourself. Cursor convenience has made us intolerant of perceived inconveniences. It would do us all good to realize the truth of this statement: "An inconvenience is only an adventure wrongly considered."[10]

At the risk of dating myself, allow me to describe what it was like to be an undergraduate and graduate student during the time when cyber-conveniences were not yet available. Armed with only a topic, I entered the university library to begin my search at that historic relic of research—the card catalogue. For those under the age of thirty, a "card catalog" is a cabinet of file drawers containing alphabetically ordered 3" x 5" cards of authors, subjects, and titles. The research process looked like this:

First, I thumbed through these cards to find the one containing information and location of the book I was looking for. I'd

9. Mike Yacconelli, *Dangerous Wonder* (Colorado Springs: Navpress, 2003), 25.
10. G. K. Chesterton, *On Running After One's Hat and Other Whimsies* (New York: Robert M. McBride & Company, 1933), 6.

scribble down the Dewey Decimal number of the shelf that held the book and refile the card.

Next, I entered the maze of bookshelves and craned my neck to scan the spines of book titles and their Dewey Decimals. When I finally located the dusty book, the rigors of reading hundreds of pages of sometimes dull and uninteresting material was a given in order to find a single paragraph containing the nugget of information I sought—a moment of eureka.

Looking back years later, I have come to realize that the search itself was often as important as the object of the search. It was as if something or someone was searching for me with the same curiosity that I possessed. Though separated by decades or even centuries from these authors with their mutual questions about life, I could almost feel their presence and passion during my quest. I was like Indiana Jones seeking a lost treasure.

I believe that God loves the child's game of hide and seek. Like a magician mesmerizes an audience, it's "now you see it, now you don't." He is the one responsible for the *wondering* that leads to *wandering*, which leads to even more *wondering*. Proverbs says, *"God delights in concealing things; scientists delight in discovering things"* (Proverbs 25:2 MSG). God doesn't hide anything *from* us, but He certainly does hide things *for* us.

God isn't hidden because we are too dull-witted to find Him,

or because we are not "spiritual" enough.

He hides for His own undisclosed reasons, and

He reveals Himself for His own reasons.

Isaiah echoes this conundrum: *"Truly, you are a God who hides himself, O God of Israel, the Savior"* (Isaiah 45:15). The fact that God hides Himself in the midst of revealing Himself is paradoxical evidence of His reality. Presence in perceived absence is the vehicle of His self-disclosure. God isn't hidden because we are too dull-witted to find Him, or because we are not "spiritual" enough. He hides for His own undisclosed reasons, and He reveals Himself for His own reasons. Otherwise, God would not be God. He is more than a projection of our own religious concepts and desires.

Christian vernacular describes one's conversion as us "finding the Lord." However, the lyrics of the hymn "Amazing Grace" frame it differently: "I once was lost but now I'm found." Who searched for whom? I found God, or He found me, when I was a small child, but I still haven't found all He has hidden for me. In the words of Bono and U2, "I still haven't found what I'm looking for."

A first-century rock star of sorts named Paul described his attempts to comprehend the incomprehensible when he wrote of the *"unsearchable riches of Christ"* (Ephesians 3:8). I am not sure that Paul, the man responsible for producing two-thirds of the New Testament, fully understood everything that was dictated to him by inspiration. That statement may sound disrespectful, but think about how you can hear him evolving in his understanding through each of his letters. Read his recounting to the Corinthians of his out-of-body experience:

> *Fourteen years ago I was taken up to heaven for a visit. Don't ask me whether my body was there or just my spirit, for I don't know; only God can answer that. But anyway, there I was in paradise, and heard things so astounding that they are beyond a man's power to describe or put in words (and anyway I am not allowed to tell them to others).*
>
> (2 Corinthians 12:2–4 TLB)

Paul realized that over-explanation tends to rob us of astonishment, reducing the *Logos*—the words of God—to mere logic, and thereby suppressing the mystic in all of us.

Even Job, a sage of his era, struggled to understand his bundle of conundrums in the broader context of God's infinite intentions. Job would go from riches to rags and then from rags to riches. His life reflected triumph and tragedy, always wrestling with the gnawing question that just won't go away—*why?* He eventually resigned himself to the fact that he only understood *"the mere edges of His ways"* (Job 26:14 NKJV). Philip Yancey writes, "Faith means believing in advance what will only make sense in reverse."[11] We make a wrong assumption by thinking the writers of Scripture had a handle on the truth that flowed through them. They wrestled with what they were writing just as we wrestle to understand what they wrote.

God could easily send you a "link" so you could "download" what you're after, but that would cheat you out of the divine odyssey He has prepared for you. Satisfaction and easy discoveries sabotage the search instinct.

In Jeremiah, God says, *"You will seek me and find me, when you seek me with all your heart"* (Jeremiah 29:13), but when you do, you will discover that He likes the game of tag as well—appearing and disappearing in the most unlikely places just to keep you searching. There are no search engines of any kind that will even begin to find everything we are looking for. God could easily send you a "link" so you could "download" what you're after, but that would cheat you out of the divine odyssey He has prepared for you. Satisfaction and easy discoveries sabotage the search instinct.

Years before the advent of GPS, I received a call from one of my sons who was lost. He knew I had been where he was and he trusted his father's considerable navigational skills. I proceeded to

11. Philip Yancey, *Where Is God When It Hurts?* (Grand Rapids, MI: Zondervan Publishing House, 1990), 160.

tell him the route with detailed highway numbers and landmarks to insure a seamless and timely arrival. About an hour later, my phone rang again and I heard a measure of frustration in my son's voice. I asked him to describe where he was, but I didn't recognize anything he was telling me. So I repeated the directions I had previously given to him, hopeful that he would find his way. An hour later he called and said, "Dad, I'm lost!" In that moment I heard a voice within, and said to him, "It's amazing what you find when you're lost that you were not looking for."

Those words came from experience. As an itinerant speaker, travel is a weekly part of my life. Depending on the year, I usually average between 150,000 and 200,000 miles of travel. Most of it is by plane, so I don't have to concern myself with navigation in the same way that the pilot does, but I still have to calculate for time and traffic to arrive at the airport. When I am driving to an engagement, like most people, I am consulting navigation apps to determine the shortest distance to my destination. During rush hour in our city, it can take up to forty minutes to travel fifteen miles. Time is so valuable to all of us, we are always looking for the shortcuts. I am a big fan of GPS and real-time traffic reports because I was raised to respect the time of others and I always like to arrive on time. But I have discovered over the years that my obsession with momentum can cause me to miss significant moments.

It is human nature to want to get to where we are going as quickly as possible. But sometimes *we are driven to expedite the process at the expense of the experience.* I think it's called the "rat race" for a reason. The constant competitive stimulus to get somewhere before anyone else creates a maze of misunderstanding as to what life is all about. Do you ever find yourself running late, sitting in traffic gridlock as your eyes twitch back and forth from the car in front of you and your clock? Your car creeps forward, a few feet at a time, and your mind is racing, trying to think of a course correction that will get you to your destination sooner. Or have you ever been lost in a new city and find yourself driving faster and more erratically? Like my son, you might be amazed at what you will find when you are lost or late, things that you otherwise would never have known existed.

I have made connections with amazing people and *had life-changing experiences due to His taking me on a circuitous route. My impetuous nature is to circumvent obstacles, but that often causes me to miss the rendezvous that God had for me.*

We were taught in geometry that the closest distance between two points is a straight line. When God is involved, that theorem does not seem to be true. His leading can be circuitous rather than direct, involving delays that we interpret as denials. In my own life, I have made connections with amazing people and had life-changing experiences due to His taking me on a circuitous route. My impetuous nature is to circumvent obstacles, but that often causes me to miss the rendezvous that God had for me. Jesus, on the other hand, never seemed to be in a hurry and was even condemned for being late! (See John 11:21.) The next time you have a meltdown over being late or lost, pay attention! God may be taking you the long way around for a reason.

Time Is the Tyrant

Characters in TV sitcoms often solve their problems in thirty minutes, even less if you consider the commercials. We seem to have the same standards for our own lives. And *wanting things faster* is by no means a new phenomenon. The Polaroid instant camera was invented in 1948, the same year that the first McDonald's introduced us to the concept of fast food. Around the same time, the microwave oven became a fixture in most kitchens.

I still remember well the Heinz ketchup ads with Carly Simon singing "Anticipation," and watching the thick red paste ooze from the bottle like molasses. The advent of plastic squeeze bottles has robbed us of even the anticipation of pouring ketchup.

This impetuous pace has all but destroyed our ability to be fully present at any given moment. Unwittingly, we've become hostages to timelines and deadlines. It has always been interesting to me that we refer to due dates on our calendars as "deadlines." Historically, the word *deadline* was first used to refer to a line drawn in a prison yard, beyond which the prisoners would be shot if they wandered too far. (I know I missed more than one deadline when delivering this manuscript to the publisher!)

And did you know that the Greek word for *time* is *chronos* (think "chronology"), derived from Cronus, a Titan god? In Grecian mythology, he was the god of time and the ages, and had a reputation for destroying and devouring. He ruled the cosmos during the so-called Golden Age, after castrating and deposing his father, Uranus, or Ouranos, god of the sky. In fear of a prophecy that he would be overthrown by his own son, Zeus, Cronos swallowed each of his children as soon as they were born. Although a myth, it's a compelling image of how time has a way of devouring whatever we give birth to as soon as it is born.

Solomon was a king with impressive wisdom and colossal wealth. Yet he, too, was a slave to time. You can hear the tension over the process of life and his perspective on time pulsating in the words of the aging sage.

> *For everything there is a season, and a time for every matter under heaven:*
> *a time to be born, and a time to die;*
> *a time to plant, and a time to pluck up what is planted;*
> *a time to kill, and a time to heal;*
> *a time to break down, and a time to build up;*
> *a time to weep, and a time to laugh;*

a time to mourn, and a time to dance;
a time to cast away stones, and a time to gather stones
together;
a time to embrace, and a time to refrain from embracing;
a time to seek, and a time to lose;
a time to keep, and a time to cast away;
a time to tear, and a time to sew;
a time to keep silence, and a time to speak;
a time to love, and a time to hate;
a time for war, and a time for peace.
What gain has the worker from his toil? I have seen the busi-
ness that God has given to the children of man to be busy with.
He has made everything beautiful in its time. Also, he has put
eternity into man's heart, yet so that he cannot find out what
God has done from the beginning to the end.

(Ecclesiastes 3:1–11)

Solomon mentions time, time, and time again, and finally comes to terms with God taking both the lovely and the unlovely events in life, and weaving them in to a tapestry of truth-making *"everything beautiful in its time."*

Is time really on our side, or is it our daily nemesis? We set the clock, watch the clock, try to beat the clock, and punch the clock at the end of every day. Think of it, we probably wouldn't wear a watch if we weren't dying. In our finite existence, we measure time in seconds, minutes, hours, days, weeks, months, years, decades, centuries, and millennia. However, God doesn't live in time; He lives in eternity. *"A thousand years in your sight are like a day that has just gone by"* (Psalm 90:4 NIV). That is a dizzying calculation of time isn't it? From God's perspective, it wasn't two thousand years ago that Jesus was here, but just the day before yesterday. And creation didn't occur six thousand years ago, but on the first day of the week.

Probably the greatest demonstration of God's love and desire to connect with us was the creation of time. He didn't want to be God all by Himself, with only Himself as company. He wanted to be *Emmanuel*—"God with us"—instead of "God somewhere out there." He, being infinite, knew that He would have to create and live within time in order to relate to our finiteness. The marketing description for Robert Farrar Capon's *Genesis, the Movie*, reads, "The creation story stands as one of the most famous and familiar in Scripture…. But…most of us misconstrue it. The reason? We have fallen into the habit of reading Genesis the way we read all of Scripture—as a manual of religious instructions."[12] Capon suggests we should instead watch the Bible as a historical movie whose director is God.

> "When you watch a movie," [Capon] says, "you never ask questions about whether the events depicted actually happened. Instead, you accept the history the director shows you on the screen." And, as Capon points out, we typically suspend judgment of a film until we've seen all of it, letting later scenes inform and enrich earlier ones. That, he says, is exactly how we need to see Genesis—as just the beginning of the whole movie of Scripture.[13]

There is a very practical reason that God created the earth in six twenty-four-hour intervals. He certainly did not *need* six twenty-four-hour days to create the earth. In His creative prowess, He could have done it six seconds! But He didn't create everything in the material world with one sweep of His omnipotent wand. He didn't even do it overnight. Eternity has no past or future, so it is not to be measured or understood in the length of one's existence, but in the *quality* of one's existence. Time may not seem to be "on

---

12. Quoted in marketing copy for Robert Farrar Capon, *Genesis, the Movie* (Grand Rapids, MI: Wm. B. Eerdman's Publishing, Co., 2003), https://www. amazon.com/Genesis-Mr-Robert-Farrar-Capon/dp/0802863256 (accessed May 1, 2017).
13. Ibid.

your side," but eternity will come when you remember that eternity is not somewhere "out there," but here in your heart. God's intent is not for us to live for the promised reward of eternity someday, but to live each day in the reality of eternity in the here and now.

God's intent is not for us to live for the promised reward of eternity someday, but to live each day in the reality of eternity in the here and now.

Paul Tillich, in his work *The Eternal Now*, addressed the difficulty we experience in relating to eternity in our finiteness.

> The mystery of the future and the mystery of the past are united in the mystery of the present. Our time, the time we have, is the time in which we have "presence." But how can we have "presence"? Is not the present moment gone when we think of it? Is not the present the ever-moving boundary line between past and future? But a moving boundary is not a place to stand upon. If nothing were given to us except the "no more" of the past and the "not yet" of the future, we would not have anything. We could not speak of the time that is our time; we would not have "presence."[14]

The description of the earth in Genesis 1 is chaotic, if nothing else, revealing that the Creator does His best work in the midst of chaos. "*The earth was without form and empty, and darkness was over the face of the deep. And the Spirit of God was hovering over the face of the waters*" (Genesis 1:2). I like *The Message* version as well: "*Earth was a soup of nothingness, a bottomless emptiness, an inky blackness. God's Spirit brooded like a bird above the watery abyss.*" That was at the dawn of time, but it could also describe our current lives while

---

14. Paul Tillich, *The Eternal Now* (New York: Charles Scribner's Sons, 1963), 141.

we wait on the Creator to speak and bring sense and symmetry to our existence in time.

With each successive day of creation, there was an evolving from formless to form. He started by separating the light from the darkness, then the water from the dry land. The creation account was given to us for more than a case against Darwin's theory of evolution. It was also to show us how to steward the eternal in this time-space dimension. That may all sound very ethereal and unrelated to a life that is cluttered by stacks of mail, receipts, and files—all the things that remind us that life requires some measure of order and organization.

Some days I deal with it rather well, but on other days the word "overwhelmed" does not even begin to describe how I feel. The rivers of responsibility and oceans of obligations can overflow their banks at times, but I can set boundaries by not allowing them to flood the rest of my world. I can do that by mimicking His creativity.

Overcoming Time with Creativity

The first thing ever written about God is that He is creative. He made man in His very likeness and image. We, too, were created to be creative. The source of all humanity was and is a Creator, so creativity is in your very DNA. *Creativity* is a word that describes anyone with a pulse—not just poets, artists, musicians, or scientists. God said,

> *Let us make a man—someone like ourselves, to be the master of all life upon the earth and in the skies and in the seas.... And God blessed them and told them, "Multiply and fill the earth and subdue it; you are masters...".*
>
> (Genesis 1:26, 28 TLB)

God's original mandate for man, which He has not rescinded, is to take dominion. The original creation was plunged into chaos due to man's rebellion, and now we are to recover the latent power through the process of reordering our "world." We are to engage in the process of turning our "wasteland," the topography of a life that may seem to have been wasted, into a place of fruitfulness. *"The heavens are the LORD's heavens, but the earth he has given to the children of man"* (Psalm 115:16).

Living the dominion mandate is learning how to say *no* to some things, because it is the only way to find what you should be to saying *yes* to. You have been given dominion, and He will not it take back from you. Your life was intended to be a garden of fruitfulness, not a wilderness of confusion and complexity. God is not the author of confusion but of peace. When trouble is at high tide, be assured that the waters will only reach so far.

> *Living the dominion mandate is learning how to say* *no to some things, because it is the only way to find what you should be to saying yes to.*

Is it possible, in the grandiose cosmic description of creation, that we have overlooked a very simple yet important phrase for us as humans? God ended every day of creation by agreeing that *"it was good."* At the end of each day of creation, even though many things were still unfinished, God still saw that *"it was good."* I am sure that like me, you are aware at the end of the day of all your unfinished tasks. Perfectionists especially have the unhealthy propensity to fixate on the unfinished rather than on the finished. Our creative juices dry up when we do this. We must be able to say, "This is good!"

It is counterintuitive for us to accept that a perfect God could create an imperfect planet or imperfect people. Yet a perfect God of unconditional love created imperfection because it was the perfect thing for Him to do. God is not distracted or obsessed by what we are not as we are forming; instead, He is focused on what we will become.

> We often say, "I am not very happy. I am not content with the way my life is going. I am not really joyful or peaceful, but I don't know how things can be different, and I guess I have to be realistic and accept my life as it is." It is this mood of resignation that prevents us from actively search-ing for the life of the Spirit.[15]

It is easy to obsess over the feeling that you are going nowhere. The soundtrack in your head is constantly playing the lyrics: "By now I should have finished my education, been married, fin-ished my book, et cetera." The unfinished taunts and haunts us. Exasperated, we fixate on where we should be instead of where we are.

A minor phonetic adjustment in your feelings of going "nowhere" is to be content "here and now." Eugene Peterson sums it up by saying, "Hurry is a form of violence practiced on time. But time is sacred."[16] The One who lives simultaneously both outside and inside of time redeems and reconciles all that seems to be lost in time. Or, as Og Mandino said, "There is an immeasurable dis-tance between late and too late."[17]

The Way God Creates

We have much to learn not just from the fact that God is cre-ative, but also from the *way* He creates: slowly, from seeds. The first book of the Bible is Genesis, which means "beginnings." God could have instantly populated the planet, but instead His

---

15. Henri Nouwen, *Making All Things New Again: An Invitation to the Spiritual Life* (New York: HarperCollins Publishers, 1981), 22.
16. Eugene Peterson, Twitter post, February 21, 2015, 4:14 p.m. http://twitter.com/PetersonDaily.
17. Og Mandino, *The Greatest Salesman in the World, Part 2: The End of the Story* (New York: Bantam Books, 1988), 85.

purposes for us would start with a man and a woman in whom the seed of all humanity resided. From this first couple in Genesis, all generations of the earth would come forth. They were the seed from which mankind's family tree would grow. The first chapters of Scripture are more than a recounting of ancient history, they are the script for our lives, emphasizing seed again and again.

From the grain growing in the field to fish swimming in the sea, all came from a seed and carry within them a seed, or the ability to regenerate. God has not created anything new in six thousand years. Our planet has perpetuated by replenishing itself through the medium of the seed.

Look around you at the people, the trees, even the clothes on your body—they all came from the original seed of God's prolific word. In every bird there is a flock of birds; in every fish there is a school of fish; in every horse there is a herd of horses; in every kernel of wheat there are endless fields of grain; in every acorn a forest of oaks; and so on. More importantly, you came from a seed and carry within you innumerable seeds waiting to come to life through your life.

If purpose is the fruit of meaning in life, then it starts with a seed that *goes* through and *grows* through a process. Our culture is results-oriented and tends to forget that everything we are or have comes from a seed, whether it is natural, spiritual, mental, emotional, or relational. And since seeds are small, their growth is absolutely essential to life. The oldest tree in the world, located in Sweden, is estimated to be more than nine thousand years old. And it is still growing! A tree never stops growing until it dies. Think of that the next time you stand under a towering oak tree that is decades old. No matter how tall it is, or how far its branches are extended, it is still growing. As long as it is alive, it is constantly reaching upward and outward.

Many years ago I visited Burney Falls in northern California and saw something that I will never forget. I came upon a cross section of a ponderosa pine where each of its many, many rings were carefully delineated. Each of its many rings corresponded to its years of growth and, different in color and pattern, reflected what had happened over time. The geologist had pointed out that the differences in the rings indicated years when there had been droughts, floods, pestilence, earthquakes, and so on.

Isaiah said, *"Like the days of a tree shall the days of my people be"* (Isaiah 65:22). Our growth, like the tree, is impacted by how we grow through seasons of dryness, abundance, and persecution. The strength and stature of that ponderosa pine was encoded in its core. The "Lord of the rings" is the Geologist. He never allows us just to *go* through seasons but to *grow* through them.

In the Far East there is a remarkable tree called the Chinese bamboo tree. This tree is different from most trees in that it doesn't grow in the usual fashion. For four years, it grows only underground, spreading its root system. Then, in the fifth year, an amazing thing happens—the tree begins to grow at an astonishing rate. In a period of just five weeks, a Chinese bamboo tree can grow to a height of ninety feet. It's almost as if you can actually *see* the tree growing before your very eyes. What is happening during those years of dormancy? Unseen, the bamboo tree's roots are tunneling deep to support the growth to come.

Growth that happens at the deeper levels of who we are, in the very soil of our souls, is not always as observable as we would prefer, due to our superficial perceptions. But groaning and grumbling about your lack of growth is not the answer. God plants all of us in environments that are not always hospitable. None of us was intended to live in a greenhouse where the climate is always temperate. Greenhouse plants can never grow to their full potential until transplanted from the shallow soil of pots to the earth where they can thrive. We have the tendency to want to "get out" of difficult situations, but God is more interested in what *we get out of it* rather than *getting us out of it*. Deliverance does not always come in the form of being extricated from struggles. More often than not, you will be educated by your difficulties, as you endure them. When you finally realize that wherever you go, there you are, you will learn to ask the peril, "What have you come to teach me?"

Growth happens on parallel planes. Like the tree, our upward spiritual reach is proportionate to outreach. Put simply, my relationship with God is always connected to my relationship with others. You cannot separate the two. Scripture says, *"None of us lives to himself"* (Romans 14:7).

> *Deliverance does not always come in the form of being*
> *extricated from struggles. More often than not, you will be*
> *educated by your difficulties, as you endure them.*

When I am offended, I can either grow in forgiveness or I can allow bitterness to take root in me. When I feel rejected, I can withdraw and wither or I can reach out in reconciliation. When I am betrayed, I can allow the soil of my soul to harden or I can allow the sweet fruit of the spirit to grow in me. It is not what happens *to* me that is as important as what happens *in* me. Genuine growth will not occur through effortless osmosis, but it is always organic.

You arrived here as a result of your father's seed fertilizing and your mother's awaiting egg. For nine to ten months, you went through the process of gestation. Our mothers are glad that they didn't become pregnant one day and grow a nine-pound baby in their belly in a week's time! The months of your development and her body changing to accommodate the life growing within were essential. Were there to be a premature birth, the result could have been death or emergency life support to help you breathe on your own. The growth that is so indispensable to life takes, not talent, not money, not prestige, not power, but *time*. Tragically, the purpose that is growing inside each one of us is often stillborn—not due to illegitimacy but to premature delivery. We must learn to be patient.

One of my favorite theatrical examples of how the long road of process leads to purpose is depicted in *The Ultimate Gift*, a best-selling book by Jim Stovall that was made into a motion picture of the same name. In it, Jason Stevens, a self-absorbed young man raised in wealth and privilege expects to receive a huge inheritance when his wealthy grandfather dies. Instead of a large check, however, the old tycoon leaves behind an unorthodox will full of challenges for Jason to complete before he can receive his money. Shocked and angered, Jason almost takes a pass, but greed ultimately wins out and he presents himself at the office of his grandfather's friend and lawyer each month to receive a new challenge.

For twelve months, Jason submits to his grandfather's crash course on life that includes lessons on hard work, generosity, education, problem-solving, relationships, gratitude, and love. Although Jason initially takes on the challenges with much grumbling and complaining, he sticks to the plan and as each month goes by, his character grows as he passes one test after another. In the end, Jason finds great satisfaction in completing his grandfather's year-long challenge. As he gets up to leave, the lawyer reminds Jason what originally brought him there in the first place—the inheritance: a charitable trust fund of over one billion dollars. Jason's assignment was not just for thirty days or even a year but for the rest of his life. By now, of course, thanks to his grandfather's "process," Jason is a different man, a much better man, and is now fully prepared to take on his life's new purpose.

The Slow Cooker of Process

Malcolm Gladwell, author of *Outliers: The Story of Success*, studied the lives of extremely successful people to find out how they achieved success, and he discovered something he calls the "ten thousand-hour rule." This is retold by Raymond T. Hightower in his blog, *Wisdom Group*:

> In the early 1990s, a team of psychologists in Berlin, Germany studied violin students. Specifically, they studied their practice habits in childhood, adolescence, and adulthood. All of the subjects were asked this question: "Over the course of your entire career, ever since you first picked up the violin, how many hours have you practiced?[18]

All of the violinists had begun playing at roughly five years of age with similar practice times. However, at age eight, practice times began to diverge. By age twenty, the elite performers averaged more than ten thousand hours of practice each, while the less able performers had only, on average, four thousand hours of practice. The elite had more than double the practice hours of the less capable performers.

Here's one fascinating point of the study: No "naturally gifted" performers emerged. If natural talent had played a role, we would expect some of the "naturals" to float to the top of the elite level with fewer practice hours than everyone else. But the data showed otherwise. The psychologists found a direct statistical relationship between hours of practice and achievement. No shortcuts. No naturals.

You probably know how Microsoft was founded. Bill Gates and Paul Allen dropped out of college to form the company in 1975. Is it that simple? Drop out of college, start a company, and become a billionaire? No way. Further study reveals that Gates and Allen had thousands of hours of programming practice prior to founding Microsoft. The Gates family lived near the University of Washington. As a teenager, Gates fed his programming addiction

---

18. Raymond T. Hightower, "10,000 Hours of Practice," WisdomGroup (blog), http://wisdomgroup.com/blog/10000-hours-of-practice/, (referenced February 8, 2017).

by sneaking out of his parents' home after bedtime in order to use the University's computer. Gates and Allen acquired their ten thousand hours through this and other clever teenage schemes. When the time came to launch Microsoft in 1975, the two were ready. Later, Gates said, "If I had some set idea of a finish line, don't you think I would have crossed it years ago?"[19]

Jesus didn't just pass the ten-thousand-hour test. He introduced us to the thirty-year rule. After an incident in the temple when he was twelve years old, Luke said, *"Jesus grew in wisdom and stature, and in favor with God and man"* (Luke 2:52 NIV). If at this point in Jesus' human experience He knew everything, He would not have needed to "grow in wisdom." I emphasize that this was Jesus' *human* experience. He never ceased being God, but the Son subjected Himself to physical, intellectual, social, and spiritual growth. The Son of God voluntarily put Himself in the position of needing to assimilate knowledge as a man. As incredulous as it may sound, the source of all truth learned truth. The Creator of everything became a learner.

The Son of God voluntarily put Himself in the position of needing to assimilate knowledge as a man. As incredulous as it may sound, the source of all truth learned truth. The Creator of everything became a learner.

The lives of the masters of art and literature attest to *the process of slow mastery*. J. R. R. Tolkien began writing parts of *The Lord of the Rings* in 1936 and spent over ten years writing just the primary narrative and appendices. Margaret Mitchell wrote and published *Gone with the Wind* in ten years. J. D. Salinger's *The*

---

19. Bill Gates quoted in Janet Lowe, *Bill Gates Speaks: Insight from the World's Greatest Entrepreneur* (New York: John Wiley & Sons, Inc., 1998), 155.

Catcher in the Rye took almost ten years to complete, and it's only about 240 pages.

Or go back further in time to the painting of the roof of the Sistine Chapel. Michelangelo got off to a slow start. It was his first attempt to paint frescoes and he had to learn everything about the medium itself. He made many time-consuming mistakes in the beginning of the project. He also had to learn some very difficult techniques in visual perspective. Visitors to the chapel view the painting on a curved surface from sixty feet below. Michelangelo's perspective was at arm's length. The painting itself is about 131 feet long by 43 feet wide, which means Michelangelo painted well over *five thousand square feet* of frescoes.

The work experienced numerous delays and setbacks due to mold and cold, damp conditions that hindered the plaster from curing. He devised and had constructed a unique scaffolding system sturdy enough to support those assisting him and their materials, which enabled work to continue while mass was celebrated below. To paint over his head, Michelangelo often had to bend backward in such an awkward position that his neck and back ached, and, according to him, in ways that permanently damaged his vision.

As these men toiled for years on that ceiling, I am sure there were times when "yesterday seemed like years ago," and that there were "years that seemed like only yesterday." To be sure, there were days when inspiration flowed and days when their souls were stagnant.

I've been writing this book for almost forty years. Well, not on paper, but on the pages of my heart. In doing so, my heart taught me the relationship between what I had been and what I had gone through and where I was going. There were years when things were momentous and years that were monotonous and messy, times when I worked hard yet things didn't work out. But the process has refined my purpose.

Success

If we have been wrong about success coming overnight, are we also wrong about what success really looks like? I am definitely an advocate of education, but most college grads wind up spending thousands of dollars on their degree before taking a job that has nothing to do with the field of their major. I paid my dues by matriculating for eight years in undergraduate and post-graduate studies only to discover that, as I've said, many of the most important lessons in life are not learned *in* a course but *on* a course.

The concept of success, especially in the West, has been defined by education, accomplishments, accolades, and financial accumulation. However, I personally know many people who have all the trappings of this description of success but in their hearts feel like failures because they never followed the passions within their heart. Success is not a definable capitalistic goal; rather, it's all relative.

Those who have truly savored success know this all too well. Last year Americans spent over seventy billion dollars on lottery tickets chasing the dream of getting rich quickly. The sad statistic is that lottery winners declare bankruptcy at twice the rate of the general population. According to the National Endowment for Financial Education, about 70 percent of people who suddenly receive a windfall of cash lose it all within seven years.[20] *"An inheritance gained hastily in the beginning will not be blessed in the end"* (Proverbs 20:21).

Jesus, the most successful, purposeful man who ever lived, said, *"Life does not consist in an abundance of possessions"* (Luke 12:15 NIV). Success is not necessarily synonymous with excess. The "Get Rich or Die Trying" lyrics of the rapper 50 Cent may embody the ethic of the Western world, but they are the antithesis of what Jesus taught. Success is not measured by an impressive

---

20. Melissa Chan, "Here's How Winning the Lottery Makes You Miserable," *Time*, January 12, 2016, http://time.com/4176128/powerball-jackpot-lottery-winners/ (accessed May 1, 2017).

résumé or financial portfolio. If those things are the measure of true success, you would have to keep being a "success" to be successful. Success is not one-size-fits-all. Living well, laughing often, loving much, and practicing random acts of kindness achieve true success. Success is the continual search for what you were uniquely born to do. It is knowing that you never graduate. You remain enrolled in the curriculum of life throughout your life. Since life is always teaching us, we never stop learning.

There is nothing as disheartening as to be doing something when your heart is not in it. I wonder how many people reading this find themselves in a job that has turned them into an occupational zombie. You are unmotivated because what you have to do each and every day no longer moves you. You are doing what you *have* to do instead of what you *want* to do. The old axiom that we should "do what we love and love what we do" sounds too utopian in a world driven by debt and a scarcity of jobs. I am not naïve. I understand that we start out with dreams, and then life happens. There's another old axiom that grates on us: "Life is what happens after you have made your plans." If that's the case, and it seems to be the case for so many people, then does that mean you have been given a "life sentence" of going through the motions?

> "Life is what happens after you have made your plans." If
> that's the case, and it seems to be the case for so many
> people, then does that mean you have been given a "life
> sentence" of going through the motions?

Many live their lives as if they are enduring just that: a life sentence, the foreboding ruling of a judge following a jury's verdict, consigning the indicted to live the rest of their days in confinement. It's not only men and women who wear orange jumpsuits with the words *Department of Corrections* printed on the back who find themselves in prison. Many may look free, but in reality are locked inside a reality they can't change. So many people wander through life as if in a maze—they are free but they remain incarcerated with wrong beliefs.

Nelson Mandela went from prisoner to prime minister after serving twenty-seven years in a prison cell. But Mandela didn't walk out of prison a free man—he had walked *into* prison a free man. Freedom is not an external reality; it is an internal one. Mandela said, "There is no easy walk to freedom anywhere and many of us have to pass through the valley of the shadow of death again and again before we reach the mountain tops of our desires."[21] Or as Nietzsche put it, "He who would learn to fly one day must first learn to stand and walk and run and climb and dance; one cannot fly into flying."[22]

The kingdom of God is, by nature, the antithesis of the values of the world. The way up is down, you receive by giving, add by subtracting, multiply by dividing, you lead by serving, and you live by dying.

The first words Jesus spoke to the disciples were *"Follow me"* (Matthew 4:19). According to Merriam-Webster, the word *succeed* is from the Anglo-French word *succeeder*, which is from the Latin word *succedere*, "to go up, follow after."[23] Jesus was not recruiting leaders; He was looking for followers. This concept of life and success is counterintuitive to our culture. The kingdom of God is, by

21. Nelson Mandela, Presidential address to ANC conference, September 21, 1953, adapted from a statement by former Indian prime minister Jawaharlal Nehru.

22. Quoted in Paul Kirkland, *Nietzche's Noble Aims* (Lanham, MD: Lexington Books, 2009), 156.

23. "Succeed," Merriam-Webster.com, https://www.merriam-webster.com/dictionary/succeed (accessed May 2, 2017).

nature, the antithesis of the values of the world. The way up is down, you receive by giving, add by subtracting, multiply by dividing, you lead by serving, and you live by dying.

Richard Rohr quotes Thomas Merton here, and then adds his own advice:

> We perhaps join with Thomas Merton, who penned one of my favorite lines, "If I had a message to my contemporaries it is surely this: Be anything you like, be madmen... and bastards of every shape and form, but at all costs avoid one thing: success. If you are too obsessed with success, you will forget to live. If you have learned only to how to be a success, your life has probably been wasted." Success is hardly ever your True Self, only your early window dressing. It gives you some momentum for the journey, but it is never the real goal.[24]

Probably the most important self-revelation is to realize that *what you do* does not define *who you are*. Instead, *who you are* defines *what you do*. Jesus didn't promote Himself as a miracle-worker or the newest mystical teacher. Often, He would tell those He healed not to tell anyone else. His humble admission of His complete dependence on His Father was His most prominent characteristic: *"I can do nothing on my own. As I hear, I judge, and my judgment is just, because I seek not my own will but the will of him who sent me. If I alone bear witness about myself, my testimony is not true"* (John 5:30–31).

We all need to be reminded that what you do "for a living" does not necessarily have to be what you are living for. Getting paid for what you love to do may or may not happen. However, how many times have you heard professional musicians and athletes say they never started out with the intention of being paid?

---

24. Richard Rohr, *Immortal Diamond: Searching for Our True Self* (San Francisco: Jossey-Bass, 2013), 141.

They just loved the music or the game. What's your passion? Is it music, art, writing? Whatever it is, do it for Him, and do it for you.

My grandchildren are always giving me pictures they have drawn. Granted, at their age, they often have to tell me what exactly the drawings are depicting, but I am always excited to get them because they are excited and they did it for me. Their messy Crayola work may be enigmatic to others, but to me they are exquisite. Similarly, our Father does not critique the expressions of our heart. He just wants your heart to overflow with what you love to do because He loves it, too. It may not matter to others, but it matters to Him.

That's what true success is.

Wonderings

Exercises to Do While Wandering

Look again at those ten events from the last chapter. List one thing you learned or one character quality that was developed from each of them.

1. _____

_____

_____

2. _____

_____

_____

3. _____

_____

_____

4. _____

_____

_____

5. _____

_____

_____

6. _____

_____

_____

7. _____

_____

_____

8. _____

_____

_____

9. _____

_____

_____

10. _____

_____

_____

Can you see that time is never wasted? What may seem to you like a life of random events has actually been the journey that got you to the place you are right now. You were on a journey even when nobody else noticed.

REFLECTIONS

_____

_____

_____

_____

_____

_____

_____

_____

_____

_____

_____

_____

_____

_____

_____

_____

_____

_____

_____

_____

3

A LONG OBEDIENCE IN THE SAME DIRECTION

"The essential thing 'in heaven and earth' is…that there should be a long obedience in the same direction; there thereby results, have always resulted in the long run, something which has made life worth living."[25]

"If we have our own why in life, we shall get along with almost any how."[26]
—*Friedrich Nietzsche*

Are we there yet? Anybody who has raised children has heard that question from the backseat again and again on long road trips. On one such trip, a young father decided he was going to preempt

25. Friedrich Nietzsche, *Beyond Good and Evil*, trans. Helen Zimmern (London, 1907), sec. 188.
26. Friedrich Nietzsche, *Twilight of the Idols*, trans. R. J. Hollingdale (Leipzig, 1889), Maxims and Arrows #12.

this incessant question from his five-year-old son. Before securing him in his car seat, the dad told the little fella, who had the attention span of a gnat, that this trip was going to take hours and not to constantly ask, "How much longer?" All went well until about an hour into the trip when, sure enough, the little boy asked, "Daddy, how much longer?"

The father replied in a firm voice, "I told you not to ask me that, Son!"

For another hour or so the little boy was silent, then again, "How much longer?"

His patience wearing thin, the father said, "If you ask me again I'm going to pull the car over!"—which was not meant to be interpreted as a chance for the precocious tot to stretch his legs, but to apply the "board of education" to the "seat of learning."

Another hour went by and finally the father heard once again from the son, in squeaky, fearful voice, "Dad, I'm not asking how much longer, but can you tell me how old I will be when we get there?"

Journeying to Our Destiny

There is a paradox to our individual journeys. Though God is within us and all around us, we still have to journey to find Him. And sometimes we find ourselves asking, "How much longer?" The Bible is about people on journeys across desolate deserts and uncharted seas. They are sojourners, pilgrims, pioneers, and forerunners. They were not willing to settle for settling. Their journeys were not fanciful excursions to places with commodious accommodations and there were no glossy brochures describing luxurious amenities, no superhighways with mile markers, rest stops, or high-speed vehicles. Sometimes they rode on clumsy camels or dwarfed donkeys, but most of the time they set out on foot across the blistering sands of the Middle Eastern world, never sure what hostile dangers they might encounter.

Even though transportation moves much more quickly in the modern era, our perception of our own physical movement doesn't always play along. Everything seems to take longer than we expect. Our sense of how much time is passing is subjective, influenced by the swirl of stimuli going on around us. Our mood, or what we're doing at the time, and what we think "there" looks like can make us feel like we are moving at a snail's pace. For example, when you go to an unfamiliar destination and come back again, it often seems that the way back takes less time than the initial trip, even though you traveled the same distance. It's called the "return trip effect." On the way there, you don't yet know the route; on the way back, you recognize landmarks and other familiar sites, which makes the trip seem to go faster.

Spiritually, we experience change and growth in much the same way. If everything is new and exciting, each day seems to be longer than twenty-four hours. We get to the end and think, *Was it just this morning I was in the kitchen eating cereal? So much has happened!* But if we're in a rut of life, waiting for it to pass, the weeks can slip by without us even noticing.

Regardless of your perception, however, the actual distance between you and your destiny remains the same. And you will never reach it without taking the necessary steps. The construction of steps is simply a tread and a riser, a tread and a riser, and so on, leading to a landing and the next floor. You can't just be transported to the top of the stairs; you must pick up one foot and then the other, hoisting yourself onto each riser and tread. Joe Girard, listed in the *Guinness Book of World Records* as the "world's greatest salesman," wrote, "The elevator to…success is 'out of order.' You'll have to use the stairs, one step at a time."[27]

When I was young, I used to navigate steps two at a time when in a hurry. Later in life, when my agility was not what it once was, I experienced an embarrassing misstep and fell on my face. I

27. Joe Girard, *13 Essential Rules of Selling: How to Be a Top Achiever and Lead a Great Life* (New York: McGraw-Hill, 2012), 11.

realized in that clumsy moment that I had been doing that exact same thing in other areas of my life, as well. My overstepping was causing me to miss certain steps that were there for a reason.

What do we usually say when we are making progress and then run into repeated setbacks? "One step forward and two steps back." This is how we feel when every solution we come up with creates more problems than it solves. Similarly, taking steps toward our destiny is not always about moving forward. In fact, our lives might be more accurately defined as a dance than as a trip from Point A to Point B. Dance is an art form that, when performed with mastery, is truly something to behold. Partners glide and pirouette around the dance floor to the rhythm of the music, becoming one with the melody, telling the story of the lyrics with their bodies. Their seemingly effortless movements are graceful and full of beauty.

My wife has always loved to dance, mainly because of the joy and oneness she feels when we dance together. I have always been reluctant to grant her request due to my clumsiness. Although I have an athletic background, when it comes to the dance floor, ineptitude does not even begin to describe me. I am paralyzed by both my fear of looking goofy and my control issues. But that's never discouraged her from asking me, time and time again, to join her in a dance at weddings and celebrations.

Years ago, I agreed to take dance lessons with her because I knew how much happiness it would bring her. I don't remember all the steps, but I do remember the instructor telling me that leading my wife meant doing two simple things: the first was to maintain eye contact, and the second was to signal a change of direction with my hands. A subtle nudge in the small of her back sufficed to communicate to her the next step.

I have come to realize that God, being a relentless romantic, loves to dance, too. In many ways our whole life is a dance to which God knows the steps, even when we feel as if we have two left feet.

"*The steps of a good man are ordered by the* Lord, *and He delights in his way*" (Psalm 37:23 NKJV). He is not put off by our reluctance and clumsiness. He knows that for us to fully overcome our self-consciousness and experience the joy He intends for us, we must learn to stay focused on His eyes and respond to His slightest touch.

The best dancers understand that the steps and syncopation are secondary to becoming one with their partner and the music. A few years ago I saw an interview in which a world-class dancer was asked what the key was to his skill. He replied, "I don't think. I allow my body to become one with the music." It is as if he channeled every instrument and embodied the song.

Too often, dependence is perceived as a weakness.
In reality it's the ultimate sign of strength.
It takes incredible self-discipline to depend on God—
to just lean into Him and His subtle leadings.

I think you would agree with me that we overthink our steps, fearing we will stumble. If you are obsessed with your inabilities, you will ignore His abilities. Too often, dependence is perceived as a weakness. In reality it's the ultimate sign of strength. It takes incredible self-discipline to depend on God—to just lean into Him and His subtle leadings. Yet when you overcome your fear of stumbling and being embarrassed, you will discover the movements of grace. He will dance you into your destiny. "*Whoever finds his life will lose it, and whoever loses his life for my sake will find it*" (Matthew 10:39).

An Unpredictable Road

Four thousand years ago, a man who is revered for his faith was invited on a long walk—beyond the limits of charted maps, from certainty to uncertainty. At seventy-five years of age, Abram (before he was known as Abraham) was summoned to be a nomad. He was not given a map, a compass, or brochures of places of interest, nor did he have a conversation with someone who already had been to this land of ambiguity. As the poet William Blake once wrote, "There are things known, and things unknown, and in between are the doors."

> *By an act of faith, Abraham said yes to God's call to travel to an unknown place that would become his home. When he left he had no idea where he was going. By an act of faith he lived in the country promised him, lived as a stranger camping in tents. Isaac and Jacob did the same, living under the same promise. Abraham did it by keeping his eye on an unseen city with real, eternal foundations—the City designed and built by God.* (Hebrews 11:8 MSG)

Abraham had no idea what the future would hold—he had *"no idea where he was going."* Yet it was his very ignorance of the future that allowed his faith to flourish. Mark Twain is often attributed with this quote: "It ain't what you don't know that gets you into trouble, it's what you know for sure that just ain't so." The truth we discover at the core of Abraham's story is that faith and predictability cannot coexist.

While the decisions we make today do have consequences on our future, the future is much larger than what we can personally control. If we ever succeeded in making the future certain, it would be an absolute tragedy! It would be an impossibly boring existence because nothing would ever be new. The future would be held hostage by an endless repetition of the past.

Yet most of us live pursuing the security of as much certainty as possible. The domesticated twenty-first-century man struggles to relate to a man from an ancient civilization embarking on a nomadic lifestyle because today, normal life is relatively regimented and routine, providing a security in the daily sameness. Instead of buying into that cultural ideal, however, our faith should embrace the ambiguity of not knowing where one is being led, because it so in love with the One who is leading.

Our faith should embrace the ambiguity of
not knowing where one is being led,
because it so in love with the One who is leading.

The prolific Catholic mystic Thomas Merton said it well:

My Lord God, I have no idea where I am going. I do not see the road ahead of me. I cannot know for certain where it will end. Nor do I really know myself, and the fact that I think that I am following your will does not mean that I am actually doing so. But I believe that the desire to please you does in fact please you. And I hope I have that desire in all that I am doing. I hope that I will never do anything apart from that desire. And I know that if I do this you will lead me by the right road, though I may know nothing about it.[28]

Abram, at seventy-five, learned to walk all over again. He learned to take the never-ending steps of obedience, exciting or not. Similar to Abram's life, when your journey of faith begins, you may not have all of the answers you would like to have *before* you take your first steps of faith. When my wife and I started our journey together thirty-eight years ago, we had no idea that our lives would take the trajectory we are on now. We just started taking steps. Sometimes the steps were long, confident strides, but other times we were more like wobbling toddlers, taking a step, falling, scraping knees, and sometimes wanting to revert to crawling. Each

---

28. Thomas Merton, *Thoughts in Solitude* (New York: Farrar, Straus and Giroux, 1958), 79.

time we fell, however, we just kept getting up, regaining our balance, and stepping forward once again, even if very tentatively.

In some ways we need to be more like children in our walk of faith. When adults fall, we are at a greater risk of injury than children because we have further to fall—resulting in a greater fear of taking another step. We didn't stop learning to walk when we were toddlers; we still have a lot to learn. And the worst mistake we can make is fearing we will make a mistake.

My wife and I have moved eight times in thirty-eight years—sometimes out of necessity and other times to reposition ourselves for the next stage in our journey. After some moves, we felt we would spend the rest of our lives there, only to discover, after getting all our creature comforts in place, that our convenience was not necessarily that high on God's agenda. Discoveries like that are difficult for me because all my life I have had the tendency of being controlling, wanting to be in charge of all outcomes. My motto was similar to that of Benjamin Franklin: "If you fail to plan, you are planning to fail." I still believe that phrase holds a measure of truth; however, it also feeds the illusion of control. You weren't in control when you were born and you won't have any control over when you are buried.

Since this is true, why do we worry ourselves over what happens in between? We fear what we don't understand and can't control. But for all our worrying, we cannot add a single moment to our span of life. (See Luke 12:25.) "When you think you *deserve, expect, or need* something specific to happen, you are setting yourself up for constant unhappiness and a final inability to enjoy or at least allow what is actually going to happen."[29]

The quality of our lives improves significantly when we accept that there are things we can control and things we can't. Having peace when our priorities are disrupted means taking control only of those things you can control. You can't control a downturn in

29. Richard Rohr, *Adam's Return* (New York: Crossroads Publishing, 2004), 162.

the economy; you can control your focus on God's provision. You can't control how your kids will turn out; you can control how you raise them, what kind of example you set, and what you teach them. You can't control how others treat you; you can control how you treat others. Control what you can; let go of the rest. Pope Francis wrote these inspiring words: "Our life is not given to us like an opera libretto, in which all is written down; but it means going, walking, doing, searching, seeing.... We must enter into the adventure of the quest for meeting God; we must let God search and encounter us."[30]

The quality of our lives improves significantly when we accept that there are things we can control and things we can't. Having peace when our priorities are disrupted means taking control only of those things you can control.

We become controlling when we are attached to a specific out-come—an outcome we're sure is best for us. However, none of us truly knows what is best for us. When we trust that we're okay no matter what circumstances come our way, we let go of the need to micromanage the universe and open ourselves to all sorts of won-derful possibilities that weren't there when we were attached to one "right" path. I've noticed that things go much more smoothly when I give up control and allow things to happen instead of making them happen.

We tend to think of surrendering as being defeated, when, in fact, the energy of surrender accomplishes much more than the energy of control. When I have the urge to take control, my vision becomes distorted. My mind moves from past to future rapidly, with very little present-moment awareness. When I surrender,

30. Pope Francis, *God Is Always Near: Conversations with Pope Francis* (Huntington, IN: Our Sunday Visitor, 2015), 95.

on the other hand, I'm centered and peaceful. My vision moves beyond the "clear and present danger," enabling me to see more and more the bigger picture God has for me and less and less the momentary "crisis" I faced. I start getting out of my own way. It's true that if you can get over yourself you can get over anything.

As you can see, the learning curve for me in this has been very steep. But when I am winded by the climb, I have found encouragement in focusing, not on what I have yet to learn, but on what I have already learned. On how much more loosely I hold on now than I used to. We were born with our arms and legs curled inward and our hands clenched tight. Then, when we began to open our hands to grasp objects, we instinctively held on and said, "Mine!" The seeds of greed and control are in our DNA.

 We really don't own anything. We are only stewards of God's abundant generosity. When we give something away, we are merely giving away what we were given.

Ironically, the things we think we own actually own us. You insure it, refinance it, repair it, refill it, remodel it, refinish it, and on and on. They own our time, our energy, and our resources. Now, I am not advocating neglecting the conscientious maintenance and management of the things we have been blessed with, but stuff definitely begets more attention and more stuff. Taken to the extreme, it can lead to the paralyzing dysfunction of hoarding. Jesus said, "*If you cling to your life, you will lose it; but if you give up your life for me, you will find it*" (Matthew 10:39 NLT). Or my paraphrase: "If you can't give it up, you can't keep it." Whenever I get upset over the loss or damage of my things, and I do, it is a reminder that my values have been misplaced. We really don't own anything. We are only stewards of God's abundant generosity.

When we give something away, we are merely giving away what we were given.

Radical Obedience

As we give up control, we are posturing ourselves for obedience. The command in Scripture to "obey" might make us think that God is requiring us to do dramatic and courageous feats. That sometimes is the case, but remember, it's more about "a long obedience in the same direction." Radical obedience is not always about jumping first and fearing later. A lifestyle of obedience is more like the small hinges on a door that allow the door to open and close. The hinges maybe small in comparison to the height and breadth of the door, but without them the door has nothing to hang on or swing open to. Obedience is not always demonstrated in heroic acts but in attitude, in searching out the motives of our hearts, of turning over every small thing to God instead of holding on to it ourselves.

Jesus said, "*If you are faithful in little things, you will be faithful in large ones*" (Luke 16:10 NLT). Once I had the Lord constrain me to call someone and apologize for something I had said. The prompting was so intense that I couldn't dispel it. I made the call to apologize and the response of the person dumbfounded me. They said, "I don't even remember you ever saying that." When I hung up the phone, I asked the Lord why He required that of me since the person wasn't even offended! His response: "They didn't need to hear it...you needed to say it." At the time, being obedient to ask for forgiveness seemed like a small thing. In time I came to realize God was simply testing my hearing.

The Greek word for *obedience* is made up of two words: *hupo*, meaning "under or beneath," and *akouo*, meaning "to hear." Therefore, the meaning of the word could be stated as "to hear under." It carries with it the idea of subordination, or the recognition of authority and wisdom. Radical obedience, then, is closely linked to our sense of *hearing*.

This may sound like a random reference but did you know that the three smallest bones in your body are all found inside your ear—the hammer, anvil, and stirrup—and you would be completely deaf without them? Small things truly make a big difference, or, in other words, a little bit goes a long way. Or how about Jesus' hyperbolic statement "*If you have faith like a grain of mustard seed, you will say to this mountain, 'Move from here to there,' and it will move, and nothing will be impossible for you*" (Matthew 17:20). The almost infinitesimal mustard seed can dislodge an immense mountain.

So what are we listening *for*? Maybe you have always imagined that God's voice would be loud and rumbling, like thunder shaking the ground beneath your feet. But Jewish tradition teaches that God's voice is heard in different tones depending on the individual. For example, the ancient rabbis believed that God spoke to Moses from the burning bush in a voice that sounded like his father Amram's voice. This suggests that the vocal range of God's voice is not limited. It seems that He speaks to us based on who we are and where we are in our journey. He may speak in a whisper or even in a feminine voice. The God that conventional religion has shown us tends to be the masculine persona of a father or son. But God is neither male nor female; He's both. To Solomon, the voice of wisdom was not the rumbling voice of a sage but that of woman:

> *Do you hear Lady Wisdom calling? Can you hear Madame Insight raising her voice? She's taken her stand at First and Main, at the busiest intersection. Right in the city square where the traffic is thickest, she shouts, "You—I'm talking to all of you, everyone out here on the streets!"*
>
> (Proverbs 8:1–3 MSG)

Although God's voice may sound different to each individual, I have found there to be two common channels for it: through silence and through intimacy.

Through Silence

Obedience is about listening, not just hearing. *Hearing* is a passive, no-brainer experience, like breathing or blinking; it doesn't require any effort. *Listening*, however, utilizes intentional attention. Most humans are "hard of listening" rather than "hard of hearing." Can you see the word *listen* in the word *silent*?

Solitary confinement, I have heard, can be the most maddening form of imprisonment. Why? Because the combination of a confining space and being deprived of hearing from anyone else leaves you alone with the sounds that are within. Similarly, our times of spiritual "solitary confinement" can be the times when we hear God's voice most clearly. I believe God speaks loudest in moments of silence. There are many examples in Scripture of people who were desperate to hear from God, but were unable to do so until they were divinely sequestered. Moses did not hear God's voice until he was in a desert with only the sounds of the howling wind and bleating sheep. Elijah, a political refugee, heard God not in thunderous tones, but in whispers as he cowered in a dark and dank cave. Samuel, a groggy child, was awakened from slumber and heard the unfamiliar voice of his destiny calling. Jesus experienced more than food deprivation in His forty days of desert exile. He was also deprived of the sound of a human's voice, sharpening His senses to be able to hear from *the* Voice. Paul said that we should *"study to be quiet"* (1 Thessalonians 4:11 KJV). In other words, we should be students of silence.

The silence of heaven beckons us to cease from our need to hear and merely allow God to be who He is without verbose explanations.

The book of Revelation even refers to a mysterious half-hour of silence in heaven. I have heard several possible explanations for what that means, but I think it is possible to miss the point altogether by seeking to interpret the uninterpretable. The silence of heaven beckons us to cease from our need to hear and merely allow God to be who He is without verbose explanations.

"Dead air" is a term used in the broadcast industry to describe the much-dreaded programming moment in which there is no sound at all. We seldom realize just how much noise pollution we are exposed to until deafening silence invades our otherwise overloaded senses. To prove my point, I invite you to pause for a moment and become aware of the myriad of sounds that compete for your attention. Some sounds are overt and others are more covert in their influence upon us. The Scripture says there are *"many...voices in the world"* (1 Corinthians 14:10 KJV). It's interesting that one form of spreading information is called "viral marketing." *Viral*, because by infecting one person with an idea, it eventually becomes an epidemic. The incessant clamor around us is characteristic of how our culture feeds our visceral feelings of uncertainty.

Rejecting the clamor and getting used to silence will not come without a struggle. Silence makes us uncomfortable because it makes us feel unsafe, alone, isolated. We are so accustomed to sound stimulation. You are awakened by an alarm and you immediately turn on the TV. Then you get into your car and instinctively turn on the radio or start making phone calls. The high-definition and surround-sound forms of media have left us bereft of hearing Him in the nuances of everyday life. "Inside ourselves, we often ride the waves of distracting thoughts, passionate feelings, or chaotic impulses that can divert our attention from simply paying attention to God in watchful silence."[31]

When you decide to practice silence, every internal voice will vie for your attention. Your memory banks have archived thousands of recordings that contain sound bites that bite. Even

31. Carl McColman, *Befriending Silence* (Notre Dame, IN: Ave Maria Press, 2015), 105.

as I write, my mind is frenetically searching for the next word. According to research, by the end of this day I will have had upward of sixty thousand thoughts. The streams of our thoughts are a torrent, threatening to sweep us away from where we need to be to where we think we should be. It is hard to be still within, even when we are still without. Like a duck gliding across a placid pond, just beneath the surface we are frantically paddling.

Do you ever have moments when things are so quiet that you can hear yourself breathing? Or do you sometimes lie in bed at night and find yourself able to hear your pulse? These bodily rhythms, drowned out by the pandemonium of our waking existence, are reminders that God is best heard from in stillness and silence. As God said to the psalmist, *"Be still, and know that I am God"* (Psalm 46:10).

Every event in our lives, from the most ordinary to the most memorable, is a manifestation of God's will. Every moment, even the very moment you are reading this book, is holy, because God is there between the margins and every letter. "Be...still... and know...that I am...God." Thomas Merton said, "Rooted in non-action, we are ready to act in everything."[32] The spiritual masters have spoken of the present as a holy place, the place of His presence. In *Abandonment to Divine Providence*, eighteenth-century Jesuit priest Jean-Pierre de Caussade wrote that "every fraction of a second, every atom of matter, contains a fragment of [Jesus'] hidden life and his secret activity. The actions of created beings are veils which hide the profound mysteries of the working of God."[33]

The volume of His voice is amplified when you are oblivious to ambient sounds and stimuli. The ego fears being in silence and solitude. Your ego is best understood by making the word an acronym:

32. Thomas Merton, *Echoing Silence* (Boston: New Seeds Books, 2007), 56.
33. Jean-Pierre de Caussade, *Abandonment to Divine Providence* (Milwaukee, WI: Bruce Publishing Co., 1940), 36.

E—Edging

G—God

O—Out

Communing with God does not always require communication as we know it. "Contemplative prayer is natural, unprogrammed; it is perpetual openness to God, so that in the openness his concerns can flow in and out of our minds as he wills."[34] Awkward silence humbles the ego and strips it of its need to control. Do prolonged periods of silence make you antsy? That's your ego's unwillingness to abdicate its need for more words. It is desperate for information, but God wants you to experience something that transcends information: intimacy.

Awkward silence humbles the ego and strips it of its need to control. Do prolonged periods of silence make you antsy? That's your ego's unwillingness to abdicate its need for more words.

Through Intimacy

What is said and what is heard can be two totally different things. To some extent all of us have hearing problems. Speaking the same language does not guarantee clear communication. I regularly have people come to me after a meeting and repeat what they thought I said. What they relay to me makes me wonder if they were even in the room when I spoke. Sometimes what they reference from my teaching is far more profound than what I actually said, making me think, *Wow, I wish I had said that!* Then there are incidents when someone will claim I made a certain point, and I think, *What? I never said anything remotely close to that!*

---

34. Ray Simpson, *Celtic Christianity: Deep Roots for a Modern Faith* (Vestal, NY: Anamchara Books, 2017), 90.

It is important to realize that there is no such thing as an unbiased thought. Whatever you hear or read is subconsciously influencing your entire life experience. The brain has difficulty recognizing the difference between what is real and what is imagined. We assume we heard what was said, when really what we are hearing is filtered by what we have already heard. Our memories cannot be trusted to interpret meaning because we seldom remember what actually happened as much as how it made we feel. When confronted with our misunderstanding, our ego scrambles for survival, saying, "Well, I just assumed that was what you meant."

Jesus said, *"Take heed **how** you hear"* (Luke 8:18 NKJV), not just *what* you hear.

We tend to think of obedience as unquestioning compliance. We lose our sense of self and purpose in order to be compliant because we don't want to be seen as noncompliant or nonconforming. This heart attitude, however, has no sense of the unconditional love of God, but only a sense of obligation. True obedience is the act of listening and responding. It is a "leaning in" and a "leaning on." Obedience is not just about what, but how we hear. Obedience is the act of listening for the heartbeat of God's ultimate intention for us, which is love. We listen from the heart, not with the head. This is deep, inner listening that we might not be accustomed to, especially if we live much of our lives in compliance-mode.

> *I will instruct you and teach you in the way you should go; I will counsel you with my loving eye on you. Do not be like the horse or the mule, which have no understanding but must be controlled by bit and bridle or they will not come to you.*
>
> (Psalm 32:8–9 NIV)

God is not controlling. His desire for obedience is not seeking to break our will but to shape our wills. *He loves us into listening.* Dale Carnegie was right when he said, "A man convinced against his will, is of the same opinion still." God doesn't use the power of persuasion or manipulation. He certainly is capable of "talking you into" doing anything He desires. But that would be counter to His nature, which is unconditional love. He speaks to us always through intimacy.

God doesn't use the power of persuasion or manipulation. He certainly is capable of "talking you into" doing anything He desires. But that would be counter to His nature, which is unconditional love. He speaks to us always through intimacy.

Monty Roberts is the man who gained fame as the "Horse Whisperer." Prior to him, the methods for breaking horses were primarily through domination, cruelty, and force. Trainers would strike the horses with whips or tie and suspend the horse's hoofs and legs, imposing their will on the animal until submission was irresistible. Roberts studied the behavior of wild mustangs in the badlands of Nevada and noticed the way the alpha stallion communicated with the herd. The methods he employed were to cooperate with the horse's own unique spirit rather than to conquer them through domination. Roberts would enter a corral of untamed horses without a saddle or bridle and establish a rapport with the animal by assuring the horse that he was not going to harm it. After a few minutes of this, Roberts would turn and walk away from the animal. At this moment the horse would decide if it wanted to follow. The first clue of the horse's willingness to submit was dropping its head and trotting to his side. Amazing isn't it? A horse standing fifteen hands high and weighing fifteen hundred pounds submits his will to a mere man's.

The first words the disciples heard Jesus speak were simply "follow Me." Their response was not due to His commanding presence or His compelling tone. Jesus did not forcibly conscript His followers. Yet, through His rapport, when He walked away, they followed.

Following Jesus is just that. It's following him. The destination is not the foremost issue. Our future condition is not the issue. Our survival is not even at issue. The focus, the goal, and the reward lie not just in the following but in whom we are following. The essence of following is the journey itself—being with Jesus.[35]

After we listen, we then respond out of the loving relationship we have with God, and not out of blind compliance. We respond freely, out of the love in our hearts.

Dealing with Spiritual Deafness

Long before the advent of digital radio signals, I remember listening to the car radio when a favorite song would come on. My older readers will relate to this. Sometimes, as I drove beyond the range of the station, static would interfere with the song. I would adjust the tuning knob ever so slightly, trying to stay connected with the signal. Often I would just pull over on the side of the road so that I could hear the melody uninterrupted.

Like listening to an old radio signal, obedience is about being very intentional. Obedience requires a lifetime of listening and learning in order to be able to listen in different ways. Elijah the prophet was reeling from being in the wake of three-and-a-half years of famine, experiencing a showdown on Mount Carmel, and hiding in a cave with a bounty on his head. God had spoken to him in the years prior, but now it seemed He had changed frequencies.

And behold, the LORD passed by, and a great and strong wind tore the mountains and broke in pieces the rocks before the LORD, but the LORD was not in the wind. And after the wind an earthquake, but the LORD was not in the earthquake. And after the earthquake a fire, but the LORD was not in the fire.

---

35. Leonard Sweet, *I Am a Follower: The Way, Truth, and Life of Following Jesus* (Nashville: Thomas Nelson, 2012), 74.

And after the fire the sound of a low whisper.

(1 Kings 19:11–12)

A few years ago, I was going through a long period of time when it seemed I couldn't hear God even faintly whisper. It was like I was deaf to Him. During that time, someone mentioned to me the phrase, "deaf symphony." I didn't know what it meant but it instantly resonated with me, so I began to search and found an interesting story about Beethoven. With his story, it all made sense.

Beethoven was only twenty-eight years old and had just written his first symphony when he began to lose his hearing. The irony that someone born a musical genius would lose his hearing seems too cruel. By the time he completed his famous ninth symphony, Beethoven was totally deaf. He conducted his ninth symphony without being able to hear the orchestra or the thunderous applause of the audience at its conclusion. In his later years, he kept four legless pianos on the floor of his room so he could feel the vibration of the piano's soundboards. He became so desperate to translate what was resounding within him that he often composed sitting on the floor in his underwear or even naked to increase his sensitivity. This seemingly crazed composer stripped himself of any external stimuli that he might internally tune to melodies resonating within.

The combination of what he could hear in his head and the vibrations he could feel were no match for his physical impairment. His last words before dying were supposedly: "I shall hear music in heaven." I think he had already heard music in heaven, because what he composed was simply not of this world. If a deaf man could compose music that has heralded him as the orator of a musical revolution, then maybe he could hear more than those with hearing. Think of it: had Beethoven not been deaf, he might have never heard the rapturous sounds of the ninth symphony. It is truly amazing what you hear when you cannot hear.

Most of us can't relate to this virtuoso's mastery of music, but we all experience those times when we are unable to spiritually hear. We might as well be physically deaf because the tone of truth has become inaudible to us. For those months when I felt as if I was losing my ability to hear God's voice as clearly as I would like, I found myself, like Beethoven—stripped of all external stimuli, without a leg to stand on, lying on the floor wanting to feel the vibrations that give expression to the melodies and musings that were within. I often remind myself that just because I can't hear does not mean that God is not near. Maybe He was teaching me to connect with the visceral rather than the audible and the visible. Maybe He was summoning a melody that was unknown to me and to others.

Deafness is a sign that something is about to resound from somewhere deep within. Who knows, your deafness may open your ears to a heavenly sound that will transcend anything you have ever heard before. I don't know if the notes poured onto the page feverishly for Beethoven, or if they came a measure at a time. Maybe he sat in silence for prolonged periods, waiting for the next measure. Sometimes it seems that God speaks in staccato rather than in legato, a smooth, continuous flow. You hear a measure or two, but there is no resolution, and you are left hanging. I started writing this section with that feeling as I do many times when in the writing process—watching the flashing cursor for several minutes then feverishly typing, trying to capture the words before they evaporate. If feel you are you are spiritually deaf right now, you are by no means bereft of the symphony that lies deep in your soul that is sure to arise. As the psalmist said, He "creates the hearing ear." (See Psalm 94:9.)

Taking the Risk to Be Obedient

Obedience is not a singular act but an attitude of life, leading to greater and greater risk, and that obedience is the choice between our finite knowledge and God's infinite knowledge and power. Progressing along the path of obedience is not an effort to earn anything from God but an effort to learn something about Him. Whenever insecurities arise they inevitably reveal areas where we actually *are* secure. I read a quote by T. S. Eliot once and it seemed as if his words morphed into an index finger that thumped me on the chest. "Only those who will risk going too far can possibly find out how far one can go."

 If we are living a life of faith, our risk tolerance is continually pushed to the limits, regardless of age or income. God doesn't challenge you with the possible because it would exclude His involvement.

In financial terms, risk tolerance is the degree of uncertainty an investor can handle in regard to a negative change in the value of their portfolio. The amount of risk one can take involves several variables, such as income, age, and financial goals. For example, a seventy-year-old will have a lower risk tolerance than a thirty-year-old, for obvious reasons. If we are living a life of faith, our risk tolerance is continually pushed to the limits, regardless of age or income. God doesn't challenge you with the possible because it would exclude His involvement.

I am sure most of you have read this story or perhaps heard about it in a sermon, but it certainly bears repeating on the subject of risk. In 1859, Charles Blondin, a French daredevil tightrope-walker, stretched a hemp cable 3.25 inches in diameter across Niagara Falls. The falls are 167 feet high and 2,600 feet across, with hundreds of thousands of gallons of thundering water cascading over the rim every minute. The daredevil drew a crowd as he walked across the Falls and back on the bouncy cable. Then came his unexpected encore. He asked the crowd how many of them believed that he walk across the falls again, but this time pushing a man in a wheelbarrow. The crowd wildly cheered their assent: "Yes! We believe you can do it!" Blondin followed up, "Do I have a volunteer to ride in the wheelbarrow?" And the ecstatic shouts of support were turned to complete silence.

We admire those who have the fortitude to risk everything as long as we can admire them from a safe distance. However, nothing of any significance is accomplished by so-called realistic people. Significant accomplishments belong to those who realize that the risk involved pales in comparison to the inheritance that awaits them. In a letter to a critic of his paintings, Van Gogh wrote, "I am always doing what I can't do yet in order to learn how to do it." John Ortberg titled his book using a phrase inspired by the apostle Peter walking on water, one the great examples of risk-taking in Scripture: *If You Want to Walk on Water, You've Got to Get Out of the Boat.*

David, an adolescent, was naïve enough to take on Goliath's dare. His older brothers had the brawn but lacked bravery. David didn't see this gargantuan as being too big to hit, but too big to miss. Our fear of failure compels us to seek the sure thing over risky things. If there is no risk involved then there is no faith required. But when we realize, as David did, whom God is and that He lives within us, we no longer have an excuse to live as mere men. Walking with God always leads you from one formidable challenge to another.

Napoleon said, "The torment of precautions often exceed the dangers to be avoided. It is sometimes better to abandon one's self to destiny." The stories I have read of men who have made lots money usually include stories where they have also lost lots of money. The athletes who are inducted into their respective halls of fame are the ones who took the risk that their play-it-safe and soon-forgotten teammates retreated from. If I timidly guard my respectability and reputation among those who applaud me when I do well, I am living according to *their* hesitation and limitation. My friend Bill Johnson said, "If you live cautiously your friends will call you wise. You just won't move many mountains."[36] Go ahead, get in the wheelbarrow and experience the rush and sure rewards of taking a risk.

Following his dramatic and unmistakable call, Abraham experienced times on his trek across uncharted land when he lost his divine signal and times when the silence seemed deafening. Leaving the land of his nativity, all his relatives, and possessions was only be the beginning of his test of obedience. God upped the ante with every course correction. The ultimate test of Abraham's obedience seems totally contrary to the nature of the God he had followed for more than fifty years. He had successfully passed nine other tests of increasing difficulty, but this seems extremely outlandish.

> *After all this, God tested Abraham. God said, "Abraham!"*
> *"Yes? answered Abraham. "I'm listening." He said, "Take*
> *your dear son Isaac whom you love and go to the land of*
> *Moriah. Sacrifice him there as a burnt offering on one of the*
> *mountains that I'll point out to you."*
>
> (Genesis 22:1–2 MSG)

There are a number of things about this exchange that are baffling. The world in which Abraham lived was bathed in the blood of human sacrifice required by pagan gods. How could the God of goodness and provision he had come to know require him to murder the son He had given him? Had God mislead him? Had He hidden His sadistic intent from him all these years? Abraham responds without any apparent hesitation unlike what he had done many years prior. He didn't know why and he didn't know where. But he sets out on a three-day, fifty-mile journey to do the unthinkable. There is such irony in this scenario. Abraham, a father and now an ostensible executioner, obeys God; and Isaac, the victim,

---

36. Bill Johnson, *Experience the Impossible: Simple Ways to Unleash Heaven's Power on Earth* (Bloomington, MN: Chosen Books, 2014), 51.

obeys his father. Why does an all-knowing God need to test anybody? Shouldn't He know what is in our hearts without testing us?

God doesn't test us to see what we have learned, as if He didn't already know. He tests us to see if we are still willing to learn.

A test in any situation demands more from you than you think you have. A test of this magnitude would surely cause the rational mind to say, "This is impossible. This is not what I signed up for! It is beyond who I am!" You don't pass this kind of test with understanding or with reason. In Hebrew, tests are closely connected to miracles. In fact, they are practically the same word. A miracle is when God transcends natural law and demonstrates unlimited powers. A test is when God invites you to do the same. That is why people who pass tests cause miracles to happen as God mirrors Himself in them.

A miracle is when God transcends natural law and demonstrates unlimited powers. A test is when God invites you to do the same. That is why people who pass tests cause miracles to happen as God mirrors Himself in them.

The Dangers of Comparison

We are all creatures of comparison, thinking that what God requires of those we admire is also required of us. The daring obedience of Noah to build an ark when there had never been a single drop of precipitation; the unwavering obedience of Abraham to leave everything, venturing into the unknown, and being willing to sacrifice his son; and all the others listed in the Hall of Faith who didn't hesitate when God asked them to do big things can cause us to feel like obedience of that caliber is unattainable for us. Furthermore, the obedience required of Jesus unto his death was far more demanding than we could ever find in ourselves.

However, obedience is not accomplished through comparison or replicating the courageous acts of others. All of us are running different races that require us to stay in our own lane. If you have ever seen an eight-hundred-meter race, you know that each of the runners compete in staggered lanes that appear to give an advantage to the runner on the outside who starts closest to the finish line. In reality, all of the runners run the same distance. The staggering is to compensate for the fact that the outside lanes are longer.

I think if the apostle Paul were alive today, he would be a sports enthusiast because of the many sporting references he makes in his writings. Imagine this legendary author of Scripture being a "jock." Paul regularly draws from the early Olympic Games to illustrate truth. He must have been watching a race in an arena when he noticed the runners carefully staying in their lanes so as not to be disqualified. The runners take their places in the starting blocks, crouched and leaning forward, awaiting the starting gun— or whatever they used back then. From start to finish, they are required to stay in a lane that is only four feet wide. This inspired Paul to write, *"Run with endurance the race that is set before [you]."*

> *Therefore, since we are surrounded by so great a cloud of witnesses, let us also lay aside every weight, and sin which clings so closely, and let us run with endurance the race that is set before us.* (Hebrews 12:1)

In other words, stay in your lane. Seldom does any runner lead from start to finish. The lead usually changes several times. If you become distracted by where you are compared to where the other runners are, you can stray into their lane.

I remember, many years ago, getting out of my lane while listening to the testimony of a missionary who had lived a life of sacrifice in Haiti. As he recounted the years of surviving bouts of malaria, living in squalor, and ministering to pagans, I thought to myself, *I'm not sure I am even a Christian. I could never live like that if God required it of me.* For a moment I felt myself drifting out of my lane. Then I heard a voice inside me say, "You are focusing on the wrong thing. You are impressed with this man's obedience and commitment to his call. You should be focusing not on him, but on My grace that is working through him." It's about staying in your lane.

> *But whatever I am now, it is all because God poured out his special favor on me—and not without results. For I have worked harder than any of the other apostles; yet it was not I but God who was working through me by his grace.*
>
> (1 Corinthians 15:10 NLT)

I don't think any of us are immune to comparing where we are in life with our peers. That is why it is so important to remember that Paul emphasizes *"the race that God has set before* [you]," not someone else. Maybe you are thinking that you should be further along by now. Maybe you feel you have fallen behind, or, you're thinking you will never finish. Runners that are at the point of exhaustion often experience the release of a natural chemical in their bodies called endorphins. Endorphins are a reserve of energy that have, in some cases, produced superhuman strength, enabling a mother to lift a car off of her trapped child. They are in the body all along, but are not released until someone times of great stress. Marathon runners use the phrase "hit the wall" to describe the point of giving up; when their muscles are on fire and screaming *Stop!* The will to finish enables us to press past the pain. I know that serious marathoners run to win, but those who finish run against the distance, not so much against the other runners or against time—a long obedience in the same direction.

Wonderings

Exercises to Do While Wandering

Over the next week, sit in silence for ten minutes each day. Set a timer so you don't have to worry about the time. Don't worry if your mind races, if you become distracted, or even if you drift off. Just sit there in silence. Trust me, it will seem agonizing at first, but over time, it will get easier. On the lines provided, write down anything that comes into your mind that might be from God.

1. *I Am the God that healeth thee.*

2.

3.

4.

5.

6. _____

_____

_____

7. _____

_____

_____

What might God be communicating to you or telling you to do?

_____

_____

_____

_____

_____

_____

_____

_____

_____

_____

_____

_____

REFLECTIONS

_____

_____

_____

_____

_____

_____

_____

_____

_____

_____

_____

_____

_____

_____

_____

_____

_____

_____

_____

_____

4

LIVING IN MYSTERY:
WHAT HAPPENS WHILE YOU WAIT?

I would rather live in a world where my life is surrounded
by mystery than live in a world so small that my mind
could comprehend it.[37]
—*Harry Emerson Fosdick*

*The secret things belong to the LORD our God, but the things
that are revealed belong to us and to our children forever.*

(Deuteronomy 29:29)

All of us want to know God. Yet to know God, I think you must
give up and let go of all preconceptions, all beliefs about God.
That's the mystery! God is not anything you think. Our unique
experiences with God can remind us of His presence, but their
absence does not prove His absence.

---

37. Quoted in C. P. Bottrell, *Living the Mystery* (Durham, CT: Eloquent Books,
2009), 95.

The Bliss of Mystery

Contrary to what most people believe, the responsibility of religious institutions is not to provide easy answers to every question. Rather, their weighty job is to teach us how to live in mystery. God isn't objectified by our knowledge; He is the cause of our wonder. I love the honesty and intellectual humility (more on that later) of Brian McLaren:

> I'm sure I am wrong about many things, although I'm not sure exactly which things I'm wrong about. I'm even sure I'm wrong about what I think I'm right about in at least some cases.[38]

> We must, therefore, never underestimate our power to be wrong when talking about God, when thinking about God, when imagining God—whether in prose or in poetry.[39]

> A generous orthodoxy, in contrast to the tense, narrow, controlling orthodoxies of so much of Christian history, doesn't take itself too seriously. It is humble; it doesn't claim too much; it admits it walks with a limp.[40]

Our ego has an insatiable need to know why, when, and how. As humans we desperately demand definitions, not realizing that as soon as we define something or someone, we have confined them. When we seek to define God, we run a huge risk of confining Him. God and our concepts of God are not the same, though we think they are. God is not an intellectual or esoteric idea that can ever be mastered; He is a Being with whom we have a relationship. Yet too often we would rather live under known rules—what God wants from us—than live in the uncertainty but glory of an unfolding mystery of relationship.

---

38. Brian D. McLaren, *A Generous Orthodoxy* (Grand Rapids, MI: Zondervan, 2003), 19–20.
39. Ibid., 153.
40. Ibid., 155.

I have always held the Bible in high regard, but even the Holy Scriptures are still written by human beings, in a language to be understood by human beings, received through the cognitive filter of human beings. With that perspective, it's easy to see why interpretation of the Holy Scriptures are so widely varied!

There are some things that will not translate from the infinite realm of God to primitive human language.
If you have more questions than you do answers,
and if your life is a bundle of conundrums,
you are truly discovering that He is
the Way, the Truth, and the Life.

Living in the mystery of His purposes requires us to humbly admit, as Paul said, that we *"see things imperfectly, like puzzling reflections in a mirror…. All that I know now is partial and incomplete"* (1 Corinthians 13:12 NLT). It may sound trite, but our questions truly do keep us on a quest to know Him—like a starving animal following a trail of crumbs that leads us to the Bread of Life Himself. In 2 Corinthians, Paul described an experience he had when transported to the third heaven: *"I was caught up to paradise and heard things so astounding that they cannot be expressed in words, things no human is allowed to tell"* (2 Corinthians 12:4 NLT). There are some things that will not translate from the infinite realm of God to primitive human language. If you have more questions than you do answers, and if your life is a bundle of conundrums, you are truly discovering that He is the Way, the Truth, and the Life. (See John 14:6.)

But, being wired with five senses, we can't resist measuring, counting, and naming. When man invented the quill and paper, he began, with darkened consciousness, to capture his idea of God. The Christian mystic of the thirteenth century, Meister Eckhart, expressed the mystery like this: "I pray God to rid me of God." Augustine said, "The supreme excellence of the divinity exceeds the capacity of our customary speech. For God is more truthfully contemplated than spoken about, and is more truly there than thought can comprehend." Have you heard the hymn "The Love of God"? The songwriter, Frederick M. Lehman, explained that the words of this incredible third verse were found scribbled on a wall of a narrow room in an insane asylum by a patient:

> Could we with ink the ocean fill,
> And were the skies of parchment made;
> Were every stalk on earth a quill,
> And every man a scribe by trade;
> To write the love of God above
> Would drain the ocean dry;
> Nor could the scroll contain the whole,
> Though stretched from sky to sky.

The verse wasn't discovered until after they had laid this patient in his grave. Lehman added the first two verses and set it to music.

Seeking to quantify and understand, NASA sends astronauts in search of the Source, but, in the words of Carl Sagan, spoken by Jodie Foster, a scientist and dimension traveler in the movie *Contact*: "They should have sent a poet." The church sends theologians, but their language is banal at best, because "When all the words have been written and all the phrases have been spoken, the great mystery of life will still remain."[41]

Even Psalms and Proverbs are peppered with the conundrums of life. Here is one of many:

> *Three things are too wonderful for me; four I do not understand: the way of an eagle in the sky, the way of a serpent on a*

---

41. Kent Nerburn, *Simple Truths: Clear and Simple Guidance on the Big Issues of Life* (Novato, CA: New World Library, 1996), 99.

rock, the way of a ship on the high seas, and the way of a man
with a virgin. (Proverbs 30:18–19)

What do these four seemingly unrelated things have in common? There is no way to trace them! The eagle leaves no contrail like a jet in the sky. The serpent leaves no imprint on the rock as it would in the sand. The wake of the ship disappears almost as soon as it's made. The virgin conceives and is with child, yet unbeknownst to her or her partner. There are some things that can't be traced. They have to be trusted.

> Imagination is more important than knowledge. For knowledge is limited to all we now know and understand, while imagination embraces the entire world, and all there ever will be to know and understand.[42]

I had an insatiable hunger for knowledge in my twenties, thirties, and forties. My education had programmed me to search for answers, explanations, and clarity at all costs. I had no tolerance for mystery and prided myself in having clear and settled answers for my students who were wrestling with life's questions. My ego was so fragile in those days (and I am embarrassed to admit that it still rears its ugly head no matter what my age!).

During that period in my life, one student approached me with a burning question. I remember well that in my hubris I couldn't wait for him to pause because I was cocked and ready to clear up his quandary. In that moment I heard the Holy Spirit whisper to me, *You can't tell him.* My ego's cover was blown! The disappointment on the student's face when I said that I knew the answer but couldn't tell him, along with the ambiguity of the Spirit's gag order as to why, was hard for me, "the answer man." For days I pressed the Spirit about why He prohibited me from doing my job. Finally the answer came. He said, *I was testing you to see if you were humble*

---

42. Albert Einstein, quoted in Jon Whale, *Naked Spirit* (Long Beach, CA: Clear Lotus Publishing, 2008), 214.

enough not to give the answer that you knew so well. I was learning that humility was a far greater virtue than any knowledge I had, and that my answer may not have satisfied this truth-seeker. I was a teacher, but maybe I was not *his* teacher at that point in his personal evolution.

 Most of us, however, if we would admit it, only hear what we are ready to hear. If we are not ready to receive, no matter how sound the advice is, we'll not be able to get our head around it. Even though the teacher is always ready to teach, in some cases the student is not always ready to listen.

There's a Buddhist proverb that confused me when I first discovered it. It goes like this: "When the student is ready the teacher will appear." It contradicted my assumptions: I thought that a teacher had to be proactive in teaching others, and in the process, the student would learn. Most of us, however, if we would admit it, only hear what we are ready to hear. If we are not ready to receive, no matter how sound the advice is, we'll not be able to get our head around it. Even though the teacher is always ready to teach, in some cases the student is not always ready to listen. How many times have you said, "Why didn't I know this earlier?" It is because you were not ready. The answer has been out there all the while, orbiting within your universe, waiting to dock with you. But you were not ready.

Readiness often comes in the form of "intellectual humility." The pairing of these two words sounds like an oxymoron, mixing about as well as oil and water. But its definition is simple: acknowledging our limitations. Intellectual humility is about being open to being challenged or criticized, accepting the fact that there is always room for more.

Some people will never learn anything, for this reason, because they understand everything too soon.

—Alexander Pope

All of us are ignorant in some way. Is it possible that that ignorance is our deepest secret? For years I studied the Scriptures to prove what I already believed, rather than humbling myself before the text. The irony is that people who think they know often don't, and those who do know think they don't. The most frightening thing about ignorance is how we are often unaware of it, or unwilling to admit it.

Any time we create an interpretation of God, inevitably and often unconsciously influenced by environmental and social psychology, and believe that interpretation to be God, the God, the one, true, and unknowable God, then we are bowing down to an image we have created— or in other words, we're worshipping an idol.

The early church fathers spoke openly about "unknowing." Their conviction was that the end of knowledge has something to teach us. They humbly asserted that we can learn as much about God in what we don't know as in what we do know. Today I have more questions than I've had in all my life. If we are afraid of the answers, we will never ask the really hard questions. And if you have more answers than questions, you could very well be on the slippery slope of idolatry. You see, idols are not just sculptures on pagan altars, they are also in well-educated human hearts and minds. Any time we create an interpretation of God, inevitably and often unconsciously influenced by environmental and social psychology, and believe that interpretation to be God, *the* God, the one, true, and unknowable

God, then we are bowing down to an image we have created—or in other words, we're worshipping an idol.

I have always loved progressive thinkers who challenge all I have thought to be true because they continue to reveal my unperceived biases. I guess you could say that I love discovering that I've been wrong because discovering that I'm wrong means I'm still learning. It would seem that God gives us the gift of mystery if for nothing else as the antidote to living in the mundane and the monotonous. *"The secret things belong to the* LORD *our God, but the things that are revealed belong to us and to our children forever"* (Deuteronomy 29:29).

Parker J. Palmer echoes my feelings in *The Promise of Paradox*:

> For years, I've wanted a bumper sticker that says "Born Baffled!".... Writers are sometimes regarded as experts on the subjects they write about. But I've never written on a topic that I've mastered or figured out. Once I arrive at what some might call expertise, I get bored.... I write about things that baffle me ever after I've written about them, which is to say that I write about things whose mystery seems bottomless to me....
>
> When you are traveling toward your destiny in the belly of a paradox, as we all are, there are no certainties.... Resist that fact, and life can get brutal. Embrace it, and life becomes one whale of a ride.[43]

The Relationship Between Mystery and Waiting

A whale of a ride? you might be thinking. *What about the difficulty of achievement that you've talked so much about it?* Well, mystery is inextricably linked to process. Let me explain.

Think of how often, in our daily lives, we just *wait*. We wait in traffic, in checkout lines, at doctor's offices, for nine long months

---

43. Parker J. Palmer, *The Promise of Paradox* (San Francisco: Jossey-Bass, 2008), xxxiii, xxxvii.

before the baby is born, and on and on it goes. It has been estimated that in your lifetime you will spend a total of one to two years just waiting in lines.[44] We tend to forget that *what happens in us while we wait* is as important as *what we are waiting for.* Waiting is inescapable and shouldn't be merely "so much time wasted."

The forerunners of our faith were all too familiar with waiting. Abraham waited twenty-five years for a son; Jacob waited fourteen years to marry his beloved Rachel; Joseph waited thirteen years before his dream was fulfilled; and Moses waited forty years doing a disdainful job waiting to hear from God.

Probably the most noted use of the word *wait* in Scripture is when Isaiah said, "*Those who wait on the* Lord *shall renew their strength*" (Isaiah 40:31 nkjv). He was not suggesting that we are to wait passively, just watching the clock. The words *wait* here can be related to the process of making of a strong rope—the braiding or twisting of three cords into one. Ecclesiastes says, "*A triple-braided cord* [or rope] *is not easily broken*" (Ecclesiastes 4:12 nlt). The braiding of a rope requires the painstaking process of each strand being twisted and woven together. The strength of rope is called *tensile* strength. Tensile strength is determined by putting the rope in tension until it breaks—then you know its true strength and its ability to pull a load. When God first says something to you concerning your future, it is only the first strand of truth that will be followed by the intertwining of many twists and turns in your journey. The tension of waiting on God makes us into the lasso that pulls us into His ultimate purpose. The process of singular strands being twisted and woven together is what gives the rope the strength to pull a load or to tether a vessel in shifting tides. "*We have this hope as an anchor for the soul, firm and secure. It enters*

---

44. Ana Swanson, "What really drives you crazy about waiting in line (it actually isn't the wait at all)," Wonkblog, *The Washington Post*, November 27, 2015, https://www.washingtonpost.com/news/wonk/wp/2015/11/27/what-you-hate-about-waiting-in-line-isnt-the-wait-at-all/?postshare=2761449015328760&tid=ss_tw&utm_term=.cd0e4cff8220 (accessed May 17, 2017).

the inner sanctuary behind the curtain, where our forerunner, Jesus, has entered on our behalf" (Hebrews 6:19–20 NIV).

If everything God said to you effortlessly dropped into your life, you wouldn't have the strength to hold on to it.

> Hoping does not mean doing nothing. It is not fatalistic resignation. It means going about our assigned tasks, confident that God will provide the meaning and the conclusions. It is not compelled to work away at keeping up appearances with a bogus spirituality. It is the opposite of desperate and panicky manipulations, of scurrying and worrying.
>
> And hoping is not dreaming. It is not spinning an illusion or fantasy to protect us from our boredom or our pain. It means a confident, alert expectation that God will do what He said He will do. It is imagination put in the harness of faith. It is a willingness to let God do it his way and in his time. It is the opposite of making plans that we demand that God put into effect, telling him both how and when to do it. That is not hoping in God but bullying God.[45]

Time seeks to holds us hostage. When you first start waiting, you're optimistic. But memories have a way of reminding you how far you still have to go, not how far you have come. Waiting is tiring. You go to bed tired. Wake up tired. Go to work tired. Nobody knows you're tired. Remaining expectant is an expensive expenditure of emotional and mental currency. While waiting, you'll question whether it's better to die of exhaustion or boredom. It takes something out of you to stand in a position of readiness, expecting good things to happen...and they don't. This is when it is critically important to maintain the perspective that what happens

---

45. Eugene Peterson, *A Long Obedience in the Same Direction* (Downers Grove, IL: InterVarsity Press, 1980), 144.

"in you" while you're waiting is as important as what you're waiting for.

The virtue of hope is the trustful willingness to live without closure, without resolution, and while remaining content. Hope realizes that both our source and satisfaction is beyond our present circumstances. Hope acknowledges the mystery, and by so doing, gives meaning to the process, to the waiting.

Hope realizes that both our source and satisfaction is beyond our present circumstances. Hope acknowledges the mystery, and by so doing, gives meaning to the process, to the waiting.

Waiting is God's rehab for the "quickaholic." If God always and immediately told you what you wanted to know and what you think you should know, you wouldn't live in mystery. Relationships stay alive by remaining in mystery. Once something is fully known, it dies. Relationships need strangeness, ambiguity, and unpredictability. Anybody who talks about God can only approach the mystery; no one can *really* know the depth of the divine.

David: A Man in Waiting

Perhaps no one was more acquainted with the relationship between mystery and waiting than David. By the end of his life, he would certainly discover that what happens *in you* while you wait is as important as what you are waiting for. Here is how Dietrich Bonhoeffer explained it:

The blessedness of waiting is lost on those who cannot wait, and the fulfillment of promise is never theirs. They want quick answers to the deepest questions of life and miss the value of those times of anxious waiting, seeking with patient uncertainties until the answers come. They lose the moment when the answers are revealed in daz-zling clarity.[46]

As I study the life of David, I find that he spent protracted periods of time waiting. David, the *"man after [God's] own heart"* (1 Samuel 13:14) experienced numerous disappointments and frustrations over his lifetime. He had to wait fifteen years from the time he was first anointed by Samuel to the time he became king over Judah. It was another seven years before David was anointed king of Israel. This means that David waited over twenty years of his life to be made king.

> *To you, O* Lord*, I lift up my soul. O my God, in you I trust; let me not be put to shame; let not my enemies exult over me. Indeed, none who wait for you shall be put to shame; they shall be ashamed who are wantonly treacherous. Make me to know your ways, O* Lord*; teach me your paths. Lead me in your truth and teach me, for you are the God of my salvation; for you I wait all the day long.*   (Psalm 25:1–5)

"I wait for the Lord*, my whole being waits, and in his word I put my hope"* (Psalm 130:5 NIV). What does waiting with your "whole being" mean? It means it will absorb every part of you—time, energy, spirit, resources, everything. Waiting will always cost you more—a cost greater than is charged to those who want nothing. Sometimes it's easier not to want anything than to want something and not get it. You can't be disappointed if you have no expectation.

The psalms are probably the most-read of all biblical litera-ture because of their palpable emotion. They're more than mere sermons to be read in a monotone voice. Their structure is lyrical, with the rhythm and syncopation of a musical score. Originally, the psalms were written to accompany melodies. The truth they

---

46. Dietrich Bonhoeffer, *Dietrich Bonhoeffer's Christmas Sermons*, Edwin Robertson, editor and translator (Grand Rapids, MI: Zondervan, 2011), 9.

contain cannot be fully understood without the tone and tension in which they were framed. As you read them, you feel the highs and lows, the joys and sorrows, the struggles and victories.

David, responsible for giving us many of the psalms, is one of the most colorful and captivating characters in Scripture, or in all of recorded history for that matter. He wanders onto the pages of the Bible from a place of relative anonymity. Unbeknownst to him, the renowned prophet Samuel had come to his humble home in Bethlehem in search of the next king of Israel in the middle of a national crisis. After King Saul proved to be a great failure (see 1 Samuel 15), the Lord came to the prophet Samuel and instructed him to anoint a new ruler to replace the maniacal monarch. At first Samuel was afraid to follow God's instructions, because he knew that Saul would kill him if he learned that there was a conspiracy to replace him. (See 1 Samuel 16:1–2.) This fear is not unlike what many of us feel when we realize what we are supposed to do for the Lord's glory, for which we know we will meet opposition.

For the most part, we are partial to the first-born, the good-looking, the charismatic people for leadership, not the "least likely" candidate. Then, as now, we are easily duped by style instead of valuing substance.

But God reassured Samuel with a plan to keep secret the true purpose of his mission in Bethlehem. So Samuel dubiously went to the house of Jesse. (See verses 2–5.) David's father, Jesse, was bewildered as to why this prolific prophet had come to his household, looking for a blueblood in a blue-collar neighborhood. Nevertheless, he paraded each of his sons before Samuel, one at a time, that he might discern which of them the Lord had chosen to be the new king. Certainly God could have just told Samuel to find the boy named David and anoint him, but it seems that going through this ritual was necessary to teach the prophet, those present, and all those who would later hear and read this story.

For the most part, we are partial to the first-born, the good-looking, the charismatic people for leadership, not the "least likely" candidate. Then, as now, we are easily duped by style instead of valuing substance. The camera lens has conditioned us to celebrate contrived celebrities, but heaven celebrates those who will never be noticed. But in having Samuel choose the least of Jesse's sons to be the king, God demonstrated that the real way to choose a godly leader is by looking at the heart of the person under consideration.

I don't think I am alone when I say that my gag response is regularly tested by our culture's veneration of those who are layered with the veneer of style but bereft of any substance. I have to be careful at this point not to sound as if I have allowed myself to become toxic with cynicism. After all, I can either allow myself to simmer until I reach a boiling point and go on a tirade, or I can turn my attention toward those who live and really make a difference in relative anonymity.

Most of the people that I have met over the years that are truly humble are completely unaware of it. They don't talk about humility, they just personify this virtue. I believe that it is an attribute that is attractive to God. Rick Warren was right when he wrote, "Humility is not thinking less of yourself; it is thinking of yourself less."[47] Martin Luther said "True humility does not know that it is humble. If it did, it would be proud from the contemplation of so fine a virtue."[48] The measure of our humility is revealed when we realize that we think more about what man thinks of us than about what God thinks of us.

---

47. Rick Warren, *The Purpose Driven Life* (Grand Rapids, MI: Zondervan, 2002), 190.
48. Martin Luther, *Martin Luther's Christmas Book*, Roland Herbert, editor (St. Louis: West Minister Press, 1948), 20.

Samuel anointed David according to the Lord's will, and the Holy Spirit came on the young man to prepare him for leadership. (See 1 Samuel 16:13.) Samuel had a reputation for his laser-like prophetic accuracy. It was said of him that *"none of his words [fell] to the ground"* (1 Samuel 3:19). Jesse must have been thinking that Samuel had the wrong address, or that perhaps the old prophet was senile. But Samuel was intent that one of Jesse's sons was to be the next king. Jesse consented to Samuel's request to examine his seven sons that were there upon his arrival. One by one, Jesse presented his sons before Samuel, beginning with the eldest. As each one of David's robust siblings were presented, it seemed that surely one of them would be identified as the would-be king. But the discernment of the prophet was restrained from tapping any of them for coronation. Some may accuse me of reading into the text, but the inference was that Samuel repeatedly lifted the horn of oil over each of Jesse's sons and each time the contents wouldn't flow.

After seven sons passed by, Samuel asked Jesse, *"Are all your sons here?"* (1 Samuel 16:11). Jesse's reply was, *"There remains yet the youngest, but behold, he is keeping the sheep."* Without hesitation, Samuel ordered Jesse to summon him.

When the adolescent shepherd heard the news that the one and only Samuel had visited his humble home and was summoning him, he must have been puzzled. Young David comes from the field reeking of the smell of sheep and bewildered by what any of this had to do with him. As the grizzled old prophet emptied the contents of the horn, equivalent to five quarts of oil, onto David's head, it flowed over his eyes, his nose, dripping from his chin, saturating his tunic, and seeping from the hem onto his sandals. David must have known that this was a ceremonial practice reserved for priests and kings, but he probably had no idea what this sacrament and the accompanying prophecy would mean for him.

David is believed to have been between ten and thirteen years old at the time. There was no precedent for a young, beardless boy to be anointed as king. This honor was reserved for mature and seasoned men who had been groomed for such a status. No doubt David's voice was still cracking between registers. Yet, there could no doubt that this kid was the anointed one: *"Samuel took his flask of oil and anointed him, with his brothers standing around watching. The Spirit of God entered David like a rush of wind, God vitally empowering him for the rest of his life"* (1 Samuel 16:13 msg).

Jesse and his sons must have been completely taken aback by this. Was this rush of God's spirit discernable only to David, or did his father and older siblings perceive it as well? Regardless, the liquid favor that permeated David's senses did not mean that his journey would be fast or favorable. He would wait for twenty long and trying years before the prophecy became a reality.

The Anointing Oil

A closer examination of the anointing oil is necessary at this point. It is important not to dismiss some of the ancient practices and rituals of Scripture as being irrelevant to contemporary times. The language of the Bible is rich in metaphors. The writers used objects familiar to their culture to symbolize truth. These symbols were both poetic and prophetic. The Bible relies heavily on figurative language.

As always, to understand any spiritual dynamic, we must locate its origin. We are introduced to the ancient practice of anointing and its composition in Exodus 30.

> *Then the Lord told Moses to collect the choicest of spices—eighteen pounds of pure myrrh; half as much of cinnamon and of sweet cane; the same amount of cassia as of myrrh; and 1½ gallons of olive oil. The Lord instructed skilled perfume makers to compound all this into holy anointing oil.*
>
> (Exodus 30:22–25 tlb)

The prescription for the substance known as anointing oil is very precise, and the compounding of it is referred to as being made *"after the art of the apothecary"* (verse 25 KJV). The utilization of skilled perfume makers, or apothecaries, suggests a process, a synthesizing of organic elements. Once theses spices were gathered, the apothecaries deposited them into a mortar or bowl, typically made of hardwood, ceramic, or stone. Using a pestle, a heavy, stone club-shaped object—the end of which is used for crushing and grinding—the elements were blended together.

Consider the ingredients that went into the anointing oil and the blending involved and it's easy to see the connection to the spiritual realm. The rich symbolism found in the oil really warrants an entire book. I will briefly explain each one and their importance.

Suffering and anointing are inseparable.
There is no crown without a cross,
no glorious resurrection without death and burial.

Myrrh

Myrrh was harvested from a dwarf tree or shrub. It was a resin secreted in the tree that, when it came out of the tree, looked like tears and made the tree seem as if it was weeping. Myrrh is consistently associated with suffering in Scripture. It is referenced in Jesus' life from His birth to His burial. It is interesting that the first ingredient in the anointing is connected with suffering even though people associate the anointing with a feeling of euphoria. Yet Paul wrote, *"That I may know Him and the power of His resurrection, and the fellowship of His sufferings"* (Philippians 3:10 NKJV). Suffering and anointing are inseparable. There is no crown without a cross, no glorious resurrection without death and burial. Samuel, one of the most prolific prophets of the Old Testament, would anoint David, but years of trouble and tragedy would follow the initial exhilaration of that moment when his senses were saturated with oil. David's memory of the prophecy of becoming king would fade over the years due to the constant conflict and contradiction that ensued. He would be anointed three separate times, all of which have significance. We think that David surely would have been confident of his kingship after all of his heroic acts and the acclaim of the entire nation, but in reality it would not be until his third anointing that he finally perceived he was a king.

Sweet Cinnamon

Notice the amount of this substance was half as much as the myrrh, which speaks volumes. Cinnamon came from the bark of a tree. Obviously the bark is the outer protective layer of the tree that was once the inner, green tender layer. The bark of the tree was stripped and dried in the sun to release its fragrance. In the same way, the tender inner workings of the Lord work their way to our exterior, producing sweetness and, at the same time, enabling us to weather the seasons of change. The moniker David was most known for was "a man after God's own heart." The maniacal King Saul, David's predecessor, driven by insane jealousy of the young man's popularity, would seek to kill him several times. On one occasion, Saul wandered into a cave where David was hiding. David pulled his sword to end Saul's life but stopped short, clipping off a piece of his robe instead. In that moment, David's heart was seized with compassion. Each time, he remained sweet, knowing that the Lord was with him and that what had been intended for evil God had meant for good. Just so we are told by Paul to "work out" your own salvation…for it is God that *"worketh in you both to will and to do of his good pleasure"* (Philippians 2:13 KJV).

Sweet Calamus

Calamus was a porous, aromatic reed or cane that grew by the riverbank, absorbing water. This ingredient speaks of many things, but one worthy of note is that it reflects those times in our lives when we are soaking in God's presence. Like a sponge, we draw on the copious flow of His love and peace. As surely as we soak and receive, we must release. The release was accomplished by pulling the reeds and then drying them, which produced the powdery, sweet calamus. There is no substitute for soaking in His presence. However, the goal is not perpetual spiritual satiation. Like clouds, moisture is drawn heavenward, that, when full, they may rain again down on the earth.

Cassia

Cinnamon came from the outer bark and cassia came from the inner bark or cambium of a tree. Cassia is the bright green cellular tissue of the tree. This speaks of the seasons of our lives when foliage and fruit are in abundance. The long winter, when trees look like gray skeletons, has passed and now the vivid colors of growth burst forth. Isaiah said that the days of Israel would be *"like the days of a tree"* (Isaiah 65:22). I think this speaks of the seasons of growth followed by the seasons of falling leaves. The green leaves of summer will eventually become brittle and brown, falling to the base of the tree from which they came. As they decompose, they give life to their source. Paul speaks of a dying that brings forth life. The cycle of life all around us, as well as within us, is death, burial, and resurrection.

Oil

Oil was made from olives in a lengthy process. First, the limbs of the tree were beaten so that the olives would fall to the ground. Then the olives were gathered and taken to a press, which consisted of two crudely-hewn stones, one horizontal and the other weighing in excess of a hundred pounds positioned vertically. An ox, yoked to a wooden spindle attached to the horizontal stone, walked in circles, crushing and separating the skin of the olive from the oil. The first extraction, or virgin oil, was reserved for the anointing oil. The beating of the tree limbs refers to His suffering in Gethsemane. The ox is also a metaphor that refers to Christ. The cycles of intense pressure on the olive is the process that produces the priceless anointing in our lives.

The laborious gathering of these diverse ingredients and "the process" involved in making the anointing oil illustrates how we are anointed for ministry or vocation. Our culture, in contrast to ancient cultures, has little frame of reference for receiving anything through process. And in the church, impartation has become a misunderstood and misapplied biblical teaching, whereby someone receives a spiritual "download," an effortless transfer from one who has painstakingly carved out their way to neophytes seeking to circumvent the priceless process. The history of those we revere cannot be imparted to us. The language and lyrics that make the hearts of people burn are not merely the product of man's natural charisma, but the result of an anointing that was years in the making. Your personal history is just that—*your* personal history.

I cannot stress the process enough since so much of what is called *anointing* these days is synthetic or manmade. In contrast, for the true anointing, we need to be ready to wait for the process. I like these words by Saadi, a thirteenth-century Persian poet: "Have patience. All things are difficult before they become easy."

Wonderings

Exercises to Do While Wandering

David had Samuel to prophesy over him. While you are waiting in this period of mystery and discovery, make it a point to meet with one or two people you respect and honor—mentors, so to speak. Ask them what they see in your life, now and in the future. Their words are not binding, but it can be eye-opening to view ourselves through the perspective and wisdom of others.

Who would you like to meet with?

_____

_____

_____

After meeting with them, what did you learn about yourself?

_____

_____

_____

_____

_____

_____

_____

_____

_____

_____

REFLECTIONS

_____
_____
_____
_____
_____
_____
_____
_____
_____
_____
_____
_____
_____
_____
_____
_____
_____
_____
_____

5

THE REST THAT WAITS

The Sabbath...is more than an armistice, more than an interlude; it is a profound conscious harmony of man and the world, a sympathy for all things and a participation in the spirit that unites what is below and what is above....[49]

Six days a week we wrestle with the world, wringing profit from the earth; on the Sabbath we especially care for the seed of eternity planted in the soul. The world has our hands, but our soul belongs to Someone Else. Six days a week we seek to dominate the world, on the seventh day we try to dominate the self.[50]

—Abraham Joshua Heschel

Rest is what you experience when you are inactive, right? Or so we think. The truth is that inactivity does not always result in rest. You may recline without but still be racing within. Your body can

49. Abraham Joshua Heschel, *The Sabbath* (New York: Farrar, Straus and Giroux, 2005), 31–32.
50. Ibid., 1.

be motionless, but your mind and emotions are traveling relentlessly from the past to the future. I returned recently from a trip to Taiwan that took four planes and over twenty-four hours traveling thousands of miles across several time zones. You can imagine the jetlag! And yet air travel does not compare to the fatigue of "thought travel" that takes place within the six inches between your temples.

Ministry Burnout

I am convinced, after years of being challenged by emotional and mental exhaustion, that the hardest thing you will ever do is to do nothing. As paradoxical as it sounds, sometimes less is more. The scriptural definition of "rest" is *directed activity*, not inactivity. I have met many sincere and devoted believers over the years who burned out and dropped out after working "for" the Lord. The rigors of religion have littered the landscape with the casualties of those who have worked "for" Him without ever learning to work "with" Him. There is a difference.

One sure sign of working "for" Him instead of "with" is giving in to the subtle undertow in most religious activity that projects guilt upon those who are not doing as much as others. How many activities are you involved in right now that are motivated by the expectations of others in your religious circle? Are you succumbing to their expectations because you fear their rejection? Are you feverishly trying to keep up with them, all the while ignoring God? Jesus is our example and He only did those things He saw the Father doing. Jesus said,

> *Are you tired? Worn out? Burned out on religion? Come to me. Get away with me and you'll recover your life. I'll show you how to take a real rest. Walk with me and work with me—watch how I do it. Learn the unforced rhythms of grace. I won't lay anything heavy or ill-fitting on you. Keep*

company with me and you'll learn to live freely and lightly.
(Matthew 11:28–30 msg)

Work that comes out of resting in Him is not driven to the point of total depletion. It works because He is working in it and through it. In other translations of this passage Jesus uses the metaphor of a "yoke."

Come to me, all who labor and are heavy laden, and I will give you rest. Take my yoke upon you, and learn from me, for I am gentle and lowly in heart, and you will find rest for your souls. For my yoke is easy, and my burden is light.
(Matthew 11:28–30)

Notice that Jesus first says He will *"give you rest"* then He says you will *"find rest."* The first rest He refers to is a rest of a spiritual dimension. The first rest you receive without any attempts to achieve anything. Paul explains it this way: *"For by grace you have been saved through faith. And this is not your own doing; it is the gift of God,* **not** *a result of works, so that no one may boast"* (Ephesians 2:8–9).

This rest is given without any attempts on our part to prove or improve. The rest that Jesus that says has to be *found* is a rest for our souls. The Greek word for *soul* is *psyche* and refers to the mind and emotions. The frenetic motions of our emotions are almost impossible to harness. Maybe this is why Jesus says His "yoke is easy, and his burden is light."

The yoke metaphor is rich in meaning. Jesus draws upon a familiar sight in the first-century agricultural world. A yoke is crude wooden collar attached to a beam in which two oxen are harnessed together to pull a load or a plow. The truth of oxen in tandem illustrates the ease Jesus offers of being in yoke with Him. Yokes were tailor-made for each ox by measuring the girth of the animal's neck, insuring that it would be able to pull with force without chaffing. Simply applied, Jesus understands the unique individualized curriculum needed for all of us as we pull our own load through life. One size does not fit all!

A striking example of this is when David the shepherd boy declared his intentions to fight Goliath:

> *Saul outfitted David as a soldier in armor. He put his bronze helmet on his head and belted his sword on him over the armor. David tried to walk but he could hardly budge. David told Saul, "I can't even move with all this stuff on me. I'm not used to this." And he took it all off.*
>
> (1 Samuel 17:38–39 MSG)

Finding Rest in Work

I grew up in a home that placed great emphasis on work ethic. I remember one of my elder mentors trying to motivate me to work harder, saying, "More people die in the bed than any place else." Of course he was reminding me as a teenager that I should beat the battle of the blankets every morning with passion and energy to seize the day. If the sun was up, then I should be up! I must say that I have benefited in many ways from the values that were instilled in me. However, much of it was motivated by a need for self-worth. We observed the Sabbath once a week like all good evangelicals but it would take many years before I began to understand that the Sabbath, or the day of rest, is not just a day of the week. It is also a disposition to every day of the week.

Our culture desperately needs a new a way to rest. It suffers from a dis-ease, a lack of ease. We are addicted to busyness.

Without rest, we miss the rest of God: the rest he invites us to enter more fully so that we might know him more deeply. "Be still, and know that I am God." Some knowing is never pursued, only received. And for that, you need to be still. Sabbath is both a day and an attitude to nurture such stillness.[51]

The rest of God is not a rest *from* work, but a rest *in* work. This is a counterintuitive concept in a culture that rewards "sweat equity." Maybe you're thinking about how the idea of rest in work contradicts everything I've said up to this point about enduring the process of purpose. Not really. The key is in understanding that our process can be enjoyed rather than just endured when we understand living from the rest of God.

Rest allows us to remember who we are, so that we do not get caught up in the need for accomplishment, power, and prestige.

Rest allows us to remember who we are, so that we do not get caught up in the need for accomplishment, power, and prestige. As I've said before, what we do for a living does not define who we are. Who we are defines what we do.

> I am a human being, not a human doing. Don't equate your self-worth with how well you do things in life. You aren't what you do. If you are what you do, then when you don't...you aren't.[52]   —Dr. Wayne Dyer

In most American social settings, when meeting someone new, right after "Nice to meet you" comes the question: "What do you do?"—which, by the way, is considered rude in most other cultures. Consider just how awkward this becomes in times of financial uncertainty or national recession. If you root your identity in

---

51. Mark Buchanan, *The Rest of God: Restoring Your Soul by Restoring Sabbath* (Nashville, TN: Thomas Nelson, 2007), 3.
52. Quoted in Vanessa Lapointe, *Discipline Without Damage* (Vancouver, BC: LifeTree Media, 2016), 106.

your performance, then the moment you lose your job, you lose your importance.

Capitalism has blurred the lines between net worth and self-worth. Net worth is our total assets minus our liabilities, but self-worth cannot be measured on a spreadsheet. The pressure to maintain our net worth is a hustle, swindling us out of our truest identity. But when we rest regularly and submit our time, energy, and resources to an enterprise that doesn't necessarily enhance our net worth, the kingdom, then we will reclaim our self-worth.

The Sabbath is not just a day of the week, but a lifestyle. It is how life was intended to be lived and how it works. God rested not because He was tired or couldn't think of anything else to do. He rested as a part of this divine rhythm, and He created you and the world with built-in rhythms as well. Just as the timing of its parts must be right for an engine to run smoothly, so there are timings that must be observed if you and the creation are to run smoothly. The creative cycle that God built into things alternates between *doing* and *being*, work and rest. The fourth commandment says that even animals need and deserve rest. (See Exodus 20:10.)

Work and Rest

Sabbath is not just a day off, closing shop, or wasting time. We don't really break the Sabbath; we can only be broken upon it. Sabbath is finding time to make sense of time. The strict Sabbath rules of pilgrims and Puritans are considered by our workaholic culture as being an archaic way of living. Although I'm not advocating a return to the past, it is important to stop and think about it. How many of those Puritans, do you think, suffered from restlessness? How many with mental illness, alcoholism, and nervous breakdowns? We are the most entertained and least happy people on earth.

We misunderstand the relationship between work and rest, assuming they are polar opposites. If we think of rest as just the absence of work, we miss the vital connection between them. There is a romantic relationship between the two. A romance requires two partners that complement each other—they don't compete.

We misunderstand the relationship between work and rest, assuming they are polar opposites. If we think of rest as just the absence of work, we miss the vital connection between them.

Eugene Peterson refers to this as the "genesis rhythm":

The Hebrew evening/morning sequence conditions us to the rhythms of grace. We go to sleep, and God begins his work. As we sleep he develops his covenant. We wake and are called out to participate in God's creative action. We respond in faith, in work. But always grace is previous and primary. We wake into a word we didn't make, into a salvation we didn't earn. Evening: God begins, without our help, his creative day. Morning: God calls us to enjoy and share and develop the work he initiated.[53]

When I quit my day's work, nothing essential stops. I prepare for sleep, not with a feeling of exhausted frustration, because there is so much yet undone and unfinished, but with expectancy. The day is about to begin! God's Genesis words are about to be spoken again. During the hours of my sleep, how will He prepare to use my obedience, service, and speech when morning breaks? I go to sleep to get out of the way for a while. I get into the "rhythm of salvation."

In Genesis 2:3, the very cradle of creation, God called the seventh day "holy." This is the first time the word *holy* is used in Scripture. The word *holy* causes most people to think of a strict

---

53. Eugene H. Peterson, *Working the Angles* (Grand Rapids, MI: Wm. B. Eerdmans Publishing Co., 1987), 67–69.

moral code that God requires. But that is not the primary meaning of the word. The fundamental meaning of the word *holy* is "to be set apart" or "to belong to God." It first has to do with our relationship to the Creator and His creation, not merely keeping the rules. I think the word *holy* is about experiencing "wholeness," and I don't mean this to be a play on words. This wholeness enables us to see that while we have made a distinction between things secular and spiritual, that God makes no such distinction. As Martin Buber put it: "All things wait to be hallowed." The voice of God to Moses from a burning bush was to remove his shoes (which desensitize us to what we are walking though in life) because the ground on which he stood was holy.

Eugene Peterson explains the two biblical versions of the Sabbath.

> The Exodus reason [for keeping a Sabbath] is that we are to keep a Sabbath because God kept it (Exod. 20:8–11). God did his work in six days and then rested. If God sets apart one day to rest, we can too. There are some things that can be accomplished, even by God, only in a state of rest.... The Deuteronomy reason for Sabbath-keeping is that our ancestors in Egypt went four hundred years without a vacation (Deut. 5:15). Never a day off. The consequence: they were no longer considered persons but slaves. Hands. Work units.... The two biblical reasons for sabbath-keeping develop into parallel sabbath activities of praying and playing. The Exodus reason directs us to the contemplation of God, which becomes prayer. The Deuteronomy reason directs us to social leisure, which becomes play. Praying and playing are deeply congruent with each other and have extensive inner connections.[54]

Peterson goes on to explain that in our contemporary world we can become slaves to the pharaoh system or mammon, as Jesus

---

54. Ibid., 70–71, 74–75.

would identify it, which has an unquenchable need for production. To celebrate the Sabbath, he says, is a resistance to allowing our lives to be defined by "the production and consumption of goods." Prosperity without the perspective of the Sabbath always results in a form of amnesia.

The Power of Spiritual Contemplation in Work

Is work a curse imposed on man because of Adam's sin? This myth, believed by too many, is due to a misinterpretation of Genesis 3:17–19:

> *Cursed is the ground because of you; through painful toil you will eat food from it all the days of your life. It will produce thorns and thistles for you, and you will eat the plants of the field. By the sweat of your brow you will eat your food until you return to the ground, since from it you were taken; for dust you are and to dust you will return.* (NIV)

It is easy to assume from this passage that the difference made by the curse of sin is in the amount of physical exertion Adam had to put forth. The difference is that before he sinned, what he did was in agreement with who he was, i.e., play. After he sinned, what he did was in conflict with who he was, i.e., his work became toilsome. Before sin, Adam may have approached his work like an enthusiastic hunter who eagerly arises at dawn for a day of hunting and returns at the end of the day exhausted but happy. After he sinned, his work became the daily exhausting grind of a thorn-and-thistle-puller who forces himself from his bed utterly contrary to his true nature.

God sanctioned work before the fall of Adam. God is a worker Himself according to John 5:17. We are created in His image and invited to be coworkers with Him. Solomon said work was a gift.

> *This is what I have observed to be good: that it is appropriate for a person to eat, to drink and to find satisfaction in their*

toilsome labor under the sun during the few days of life God has given them—for this is their lot. Moreover, when God gives someone wealth and possessions, and the ability to enjoy them, to accept their lot and be happy in their toil—this is a gift of God.   (Ecclesiastes 5:18–19 NIV)

The daily grind of work, office politics, endless routine, and competition—there seems to be no end of rigors associated with work. But work itself is not evil.

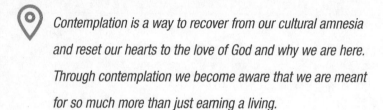

Contemplation is a way to recover from our cultural amnesia and reset our hearts to the love of God and why we are here. Through contemplation we become aware that we are meant for so much more than just earning a living.

How do we return to the Genesis rhythm of rest and creativity in our work? It may sound like a utopian idea, but I believe the answer is found in contemplation. Carl McColman writes,

> We need contemplation to slow down and think clearly. Daily time given to silence is like a "reset" button for the mind. It cleanses the frenzy of over-stimulated thoughts and feelings, and opens up a spaciousness where we can consider how to most wisely and effectively respond to the work we need to do. This is true whether our task is changing the world or changing the diapers of our newborn. Both tasks are essential, of course, and both must be done with love if they are to be done well.[55]

McColman says that contemplation causes us to remember who we really are. The consumer culture has barraged us with

---

55. Carl McColman, "Why We Need Contemplation," *Patheos*, March 6, 2015, http://www.patheos.com/blogs/carlmccolman/2015/03/why-we-need-contemplation/ (accessed February 8, 2017).

things we must have, resulting in us becoming so overwhelmed that we forget our innate worth as God's creation. Contemplation is a way to recover from our cultural amnesia and reset our hearts to the love of God and why we are here. Through contemplation we become aware that we are meant for so much more than just earning a living.

Working from rest instead of working so that we can eventually rest occurs when we are in what some psychologist call "the flow." What is flow? Very simply put, it is being totally immersed in a task, fully present, one with the Creator and free of outside distractions. In the flow of creativity you lose track of time and of "yourself," and you discover your true self, which mirrors the One in whose image you were made. Jesus said, *"For the Scriptures declare that rivers of living water shall flow from the inmost being of anyone who believes in me"* (John 7:38 TLB).

We are oriented toward goals and making things happen—trying to force the river, or even trying to create our own river. I find it interesting that the description of the garden of Eden includes a river that flowed out of it that parted into four rivers, watering the entire world. The original intention of God seems to be that the river flowed *from* paradise, not *to* it. The big river of creativity is already flowing through us. All we have to do is let it flow and trust its ultimate direction.

We've all heard the voice of panic that shouts, "Don't just sit there! Do something!" The practice of mindfulness says the opposite: "Don't do something! Just sit there!" Research has shown that mindfulness changes our brains. It increases the density of gray matter in brain regions linked to learning, memory, and empathy. Being still, paradoxically, is doing something. Buried deep beneath our surface, busyness is a veritable aquifer of untapped creativity.

Remembering that we were first children of God before we became adult laborers transforms our understanding of work. Think of the parabolic story of the two bricklayers. They were asked, "What are you doing?" The first said, "Laying bricks." The second answered, "Building a cathedral." For some people, life is laying just one brick after another—a lot of work! But for others, life is cathedral-building, i.e., play. But before you can build a cathedral, you have to know who you are and what your place is in life's master plan. The Sabbath is the time when you discover these things.

Transcendentalist John Sullivan Dwight, who believed in the divinity all nature and humanity pervades, summed it up well in his poem "True Rest":

> Sweet is the pleasure, itself cannot spoil!
> Is not true leisure one with true toil?
> Thou that wouldst taste it, still do thy best;
> Use it, not waste it, else 'tis no rest.
> Wouldst behold beauty near thee? all around?
> Only hath duty such a sight found.
> Rest is not quitting the busy career;
> Rest is the fitting of self to its sphere.
> 'Tis the brook's motion, clear without strife,
> Fleeing to the ocean after its life.
> Deeper the devotion nowhere hath knelt;
> Fuller emotion heart never felt.
> 'Tis loving and serving the highest and best!
> 'Tis ONWARDS! unswerving, and that is true rest.

Giving Thanks

As you calm and quiet your existence during a day of rest and expectant waiting, you might find yourself noticing the small things around you that usually you're too busy to take note of. Your heart will be filled with gratitude for what you usually take for granted. Whether small or big, the gifts will make themselves manifest: air to breathe, health to stand up and stretch, food on the table, and the list goes on. The gravel of gratitude works deep in us during these times of waiting.

Customarily we give thanks on Thanksgiving Day for family, friends, health, and material blessings. Yet the Scriptures are replete with admonitions to be thankful "for" what we have been given but also to be thankful "in" our situations. Paul instructs us, *"In everything give thanks: for this is the will of God"* (1 Thessalonians 5:18 kjv). Notice Paul didn't say *for* everything but *in* everything. I dare say we could think to be thankful *for* and *in* the following:

As you calm and quiet your existence during a day of rest and expectant waiting, you might find yourself noticing the small things around you that usually you're too busy to take note of. Your heart will be filled with gratitude for what you usually take for granted.

+ I am thankful for my enemies and critics, because they inadvertently teach me unconditional love and humility. As the saying goes, I have learned far more about myself from the criticism of my enemies than I ever will from the flattery of my friends.

+ I am thankful for the job I didn't get, because even though it may have made me more comfortable financially, I may have also incurred the debt of losing my destiny.

+ I am thankful in trials, because they have taught me the truths of trusting God that I may have never learned if my life was always copacetic.

+ I am thankful for people who tell me what I need to hear, not just what I want to hear.

+ I am thankful for selfish people, because they remind me that I need to be more selfless.

+ I am thankful when my good deeds go unnoticed and unappreciated, because it reveals my true motives.

+ I am thankful for disappointment, because God has another appointment for me.

As you can see, this list of things to be thankful "for" and "in" are paradoxical. Giving thanks gives you perspective on the troubling and trifling things in your life. You may not always know why things happen, but you can always know that the will of God is for us to be thankful *in* it.

I suppose that the words "thank you," "I love you," and "good morning" are repeated with such frequency that they are worn smooth with familiarity. Think of how many times in a day you say *thank you*. You say it to the person holding a door open for you, to the cashier, to the coworker who hands you a report, and on and on it goes. This social pleasantry falls from our lips mindlessly because it has been disconnected from intention. I drilled those words into my boys when they were growing up, as my parents did to me, because I never wanted them to develop a sense of entitlement—or maybe it was because I didn't want to be embarrassed by having children who were seen as spoiled brats. I think their mother and I had a measure of success in this area because now, as adults, they eagerly express thanks for both the big and small things that are done for them. Yet mouthing the words without a conscious connection with intention is as disingenuous as a politician reading a speech from a teleprompter.

We live in a rude world surrounded by people who have been taken advantage of so many times, they are distrustful and poised to question everyone's motives. The world's attitude is to get all you can, can all you get, sit on the can, and poison the rest. For those in the kingdom, the key to making thankfulness an attitude of life rather than a mere platitude is remembering that our horizontal interaction with people is a reflection of our vertical connection with a magnanimous God.

God lavishes you with goodness when you notice it and when you don't. Your gratitude, or lack thereof, does not change His intention. He does not become emotionally insecure or feel unappreciated when you forget to thank Him. He is not self-absorbed like we are. He does not demand thankfulness, but encourages it, knowing that it causes us to think about what we have instead of what we lack. The thankful are truly full, but the unthankful are mindful of what's missing. The thankful know that life does not consist in an abundance of things, but in an awareness of His intentional favor and blessing that cannot be defined or measured by what is tangible. Jesus gave thanks before multiplying the loaves and fishes that fed a multitude and before He raised Lazarus from the dead. His thankfulness satisfied the emptiness of both the hungry and the bereaved. When we are thankful, we are thinking as He thinks, living in a consciousness that we drink daily from the hydrant of His inexhaustible supply.

Wonderings

Exercises to Do While Wandering

Do you have any habits or practices that help you to become rested and restored? Nature walks, meditation, exercise, or artistic endeavors are just a few of the things that can help you to lead a more healthy life. List yours, or list some that you would like to start.

Ways you pursue restoration:

_____

_____

_____

_____

_____

_____

_____

_____

_____

_____

_____

_____

_____

_____

_____

_____

Methods of restoration you'd like to try:

_____

_____

_____

_____

_____

_____

_____

_____

_____

_____

_____

_____

_____

REFLECTIONS

_____

_____

_____

_____

_____

_____

_____

_____

_____

_____

_____

_____

_____

_____

_____

_____

TRANSITIONS: HELL IN THE HALLWAY

"Not in his goals but in his transitions man is great."
—*Ralph Waldo Emerson*

I am in transition translation—I am not where I was and not yet where I am going to be, but rather in the uneasy feeling of being in between. One foot is on the dock, and the other is in the boat. One foot is on something stationary, and the other is on something buoyant that is leaving with or without you. My definition of *transition* is "a nebulous, indefinable space between where you've been and where you are going, the place where God recalibrates you that He might reintroduce you."

From birth to burial, transitions are the very things that life is made of. You are either entering one, in one, or leaving one to enter another. If the lessons of life are not learned in a course but on a course, then transitions are not electives but a vital part of life's curriculum.

Have you heard the wry saying: "When God closes one door, He opens another—but it can be hell in the hallway"? Transitions are seldom easy because God knows that if we didn't have something to regularly overcome, we would eventually be overcome by complacency.

Psychologist Carl Jung explains that the scope of our entire life is divided into three transitions in the same way we measure our days—morning, afternoon, and evening.

> Wholly unprepared, we embark upon the second half of life.... We take the step into the afternoon of life; worse still, we take this step with the false assumption that our truths and ideals will serve us as hitherto. But we cannot live the afternoons of life according to the program of life's morning; for what was great in the morning will be little in the evening, and what was [true] in the morning will at evening have become a lie.[56]

Some handle change better than others. But if the truth were told, all of us find a certain security in sameness. Life is comprised of a series of thresholds that we must cross. Comfort zones are comfortable but they will eventually result in the inertia of your soul. When we stand in one doorway that leads to another, the time and space we face is filled with uncertainty. The word *liminal* comes from the Latin word *limens*, meaning "threshold." The liminal space, the place of transition, waiting, and not knowing, is...

> ...a unique spiritual position where human beings hate to be but where the biblical God is always leading them. It is when you have left the "tried and true," but have not yet been able to replace it with anything else. It is when you are finally out of the way. It is when you are in between your old comfort zone and any possible new answer.... If

---

56. Edward Hoffman, ed., *The Wisdom of Carl Jung* (New York: Citadel Press, 2003), 103.

you are not trained in how to hold anxiety, how to live with ambiguity, how to entrust and wait—you will run.... Anything to flee this terrible "cloud of unknowing."[57]

The threshold of waiting and not knowing our "next" is inevitable. "Living is a form of not being sure, not knowing what's next or how. The moment you know how, you begin to die a little."[58] Every new threshold ushers in a new chapter of life, and each holds unique disruptions. All disruptions tend to disorient us for a while, regardless of our perception during the transition.

The gnawing question asked in transition is: *Now what?* The assumption that there is a very clear answer is seldom accurate. We like to structure and schedule our lives, but transition doesn't occur in a box with clearly defined parameters. When we believe that there are clear and definitive answers, we miss the potential for our formation in the "in-between" places.

Transitions are the very things that life is made of: from high school to college, from being single to being married, from childlessness to becoming a parent, from married to divorced, from one job/career to another, from employed to unemployed, from having children at home to the empty nest, from being a son or daughter to taking care of your aging parents, from being a spouse to being widowed after decades of marriage, etc.

The Storm of Transitions

Some transitions are anticipated and some catch you unprepared. The unanticipated transitions take no prisoners. The events are not expected and do not follow any particular timeline. They ambush you. "We resist transition not because we can't accept change, but because we can't accept letting go of that piece of

---

57. Richard Rohr, "Grieving as Sacred Space," *Sojourners*, https://sojo.net/magazine/january-february-2002/grieving-sacred-space (accessed February 8, 2017).
58. "Agnes de Mille: Close-Up," *Life*, November 15, 1963, 94.

ourselves that we have to give up when and because the situation has changed."[59] Yet even anticipated transitions are rarely seamless. In fact, like a lightning rod, they attract storms. Every epoch transition throughout earth's history was turbulent.

There is Noah of the antediluvian world, who was given the dubious assignment of being the architect of an ark to transition his family, as well as a pair of every animal, from an old world to a new world. Unprecedented precipitation from above and subterranean artisans from below erupted, deluging the entire planet and submerging the highest peaks. After almost six months, the waters subsided, depositing the first vessel of its kind on a mountainside.

Moses, whose name is associated with the Exodus of Israel, was the point-man leading millions of freed slaves out of Egypt in an overnight evacuation through the Red Sea and then across the wasteland of the Sinai Peninsula.

Jesus made several transitions throughout His short life that were very tumultuous. He was not a storm-chaser but most certainly a storm-maker. And not the storms that are characterized by thunder, lightning, and rain. Some were the due to the collision of the cold front of religious tradition and thought with His own volatile teachings. Probably the most notable happened on the Sea of Galilee.

Jesus had just finished teaching the most important of all His parables to a large crowd. (See Mark 4.) It was about a sower sowing seed and the various types of soil the seed would fall into. As was His custom, He illustrated truth from the obvious and organic. He was sitting in a boat, assuming the posture of Middle-Eastern teachers while His students stood on the shore and listened. Quite likely, a farmer was in a nearby field sowing seed. So Jesus, as He often did, chose that which was hidden in plain sight to make His point.

---

59. William Bridges, *The Way of Transition*, (New York: HarperCollins, 2001), 3.

A crude burlap bag filled with seed hung around the neck of the farmer. Methodically, the farmer scooped handfuls of seeds from the bag, tossing them into the wind. A percentage of the seeds landed on the freshly-plowed, fertile soil, and the rest fell either on the narrow, compacted walkways separating the fields or on soil cluttered with stone or choked by thorns. In the metaphor, the seed was God's Word and the soil was the receptive hearts of men. Jesus' point was not the viability of His Word, but the fertility and infertility, or the receptivity, of man's heart.

What does this teaching given from a boat with waves gently lapping against its side have to do with transition? The truth He shared with His audience that day would transform their understanding of the nature of the kingdom. More than that, what was about to ensue later that night, unbeknownst to the disciples, would test whether or not they had really understood Him.

> *On that day, when evening had come, he said to them, "Let us go across to the other side." And leaving the crowd, they took him with them in the boat, just as he was. And other boats were with him. And a great windstorm arose, and the waves were breaking into the boat, so that the boat was already filling. But he was in the stern, asleep on the cushion. And they woke him and said to him, "Teacher, do you not care that we are perishing?" And he awoke and rebuked the wind and said to the sea, "Peace! Be still!" And the wind ceased, and there was a great calm. He said to them, "Why are you so afraid? Have you still no faith?" And they were filled with great fear and said to one another, "Who then is this, that even the wind and the sea obey him?"*   (Mark 4:35–41)

With His dissertation ended, He requested to *"go across to the other side"*—unquestionably the language of transition.

It is important to note at this point that many watershed moments in biblical history occurred when passing through water. For example, in the Exodus, Moses led the newly liberated nation of Israel to the Red Sea with Pharaoh's army in hot pursuit. The topography of the area is described in Exodus 14 as being a very narrow canyon with steep craggy walls, which begs the question: *Why would Moses choose this route to flee from Pharaoh?* Surely after spending forty years of herding sheep in this region, he knew that this was the wrong place to make their getaway. But Moses didn't make a wrong turn or miscalculation in the route he had chosen. Again, the location of this crossing or transition is telling.

Turn your imagination to its high-definition setting. Picture a caravan of two to three million people, just hours into their new-found freedom, being compressed between these ever-narrowing canyon walls leading to the Red Sea before them, and Pharaoh's army bearing down on them from behind. They had been slaves for four centuries and now they were on the cusp of realizing their freedom. God told Moses to tell Pharaoh that the nation of Israel was His "firstborn son." They were being squeezed between the narrow canyon walls in the same way a baby transitions through the mother's birth canal, leaving the warm and safe environment of its mother's womb. Transition, unlike active labor, is the storm before the relative calm that is the pushing stage. It is, by far, the hardest part of birthing. It is here that a mother's focus might falter. This is the stage in which women may doubt their ability give birth naturally and may request medication. She may worry about how long labor will last and how much more intense it will become. Mothers are easily swayed at this time and are the most susceptible to accepting interventions that they previously did not want. It is at this stage that the birth companion must be vigilant to her emotional needs and be her voice of reason should a cascade of interventions be suggested.

The many generations of living in slavery had left the Israelites bereft of their true identity. Just days after their miraculous deliverance they would bemoan the fact they had ever left Egypt, wishing they had died in bondage rather than follow the leadership of Moses toward supposed "freedom." Why would they, in the wake of their deliverance involving the toppling of all of Egypt's gods through the plagues that rained down on their oppressors and the subsequent drowning of Pharaoh and his posse, want to go back?

I suppose the explanation is in something referred to today as the "tyranny of the familiar." In many ways it is like the behavior of a young woman raised by an abusive father, who, the moment she is old enough to leave home and experience freedom, marries a man just like her father. What on earth causes her to do such a thing? The only answer is that she, like the Israelites, feared being free. When faced with the challenges of transitioning from the known to the unknown, people prefer the suffering they are familiar with. "There may always be another reality to make fiction of the truth we think we've arrived at."[60]

Now back to Jesus and the fishermen. I don't think that He was simply exhausted from the day's events and wanting to take a cruise across the lake to get away from the crowds so that He could decompress. I think He knew what awaited them and the crucial connection between the parable and the problem it would precipitate. He positioned Himself in the stern of this crude fisherman's boat, reclining on a pillow as the disciples shoved off. Among the disciples were fisherman who had launched many a boat on these waters. As they heaved the boat that had been Jesus' pulpit earlier that day onto the sea, their final thrust was to take them on the ride of their life. This was a launch into transition.

The full significance of what Jesus said in any instance is easily lost if we fail to notice "where" He said something, as well as "what" He said. The context is this sparkling lake set between the surrounding mountains. The Sea of Galilee was not a large body of water. Its dimensions are more like that of a small lake, measuring 13 miles long, 8 miles wide, and 141 feet deep. Why would this lake be referred to as a sea? Because although it was small, it could, given the right circumstances, become as treacherous as the

---

60. Christopher Fry, *A Yard of Sun*, Act 2, 1970.

open sea. The lowest freshwater lake on earth, it is surrounded by mountains four thousand feet high. Galilee was notorious for its unpredictability. Its personality could be placid one moment and then, within minutes, winds from the surrounding mountains could descend on it with a vengeance, producing raging swells.

Peter, a seasoned sailor, might have been manning the rudder, glancing back and forth from the sails to the shore in the distance, and then to the rabbi who was being rocked to sleep as the boat bobbed up and down on the water. The other disciples were probably pondering the profound teaching they had heard just hours before. Then it happened. Without warning and in the middle of the lake in the middle of the night, the starry skies that had been so clear filled with cumulonimbus clouds produced deafening thunder and vivid flashes of lightening. At first the sailors on board were not alarmed, having weathered storms before. But within minutes, even they realized that this was different than any other storm they had ever navigated. Mark described this storm as a "great storm." The Greek word for great is *megas*. The once-placid lake began to churn convulsively with swells that hoisted them up, cresting several feet in the air, and then violently slammed them down into a trough. The gale force winds and blinding, horizontal rain began to fill the craft with water. The pounding waves lashed relentlessly against the small boat's fragile frame.

Transitions make our heads swim with irrational thoughts. Were they feverishly attempting to bail water from this brimming boat? Were they preparing to abandon ship? Were they trying to get their bearings by looking for land? Were they thinking about turning around and heading back?

In reality, they were not in the throes of tragedy as they thought, but only in transition. It is our natural tendency to want to bail when we are going through transition, forgetting that God is not always as interested in rescuing us "out of crisis" as He is in what we will get out of "going through crisis." The word *crisis* in

Hebrew is "mashber," a word also used for a birthstool, the seat upon which a woman in ancient times would give birth to a new life. Crisis will either crush you or create a new you. Disorientation is His way of reorienting us.

These men were so discombobulated that they had forgotten what Jesus had said to them as they shoved off: *"Let us go across."* In their meltdown they were astonished that with the wind howling, the waves battering them, and the boat full of water, Jesus remained asleep. *How could He sleep through this?* They also had failed to notice that even though the boat was filling with water, it was still afloat, defying the laws of buoyancy.

> It is our natural tendency to want to bail when
> we are going through transition, forgetting that God
> is not always as interested in rescuing us "out of crisis"
> as He is in what we will get out of "going through crisis."

An entire sea is unable to sink a boat unless it gets inside the boat. When we allow the things on the outside of us to get inside of us, we begin to sink. The question is, who was asleep and who was awake? The inference of the passage indicates they had to jostle Jesus from a deep sleep. *"Teacher, do you not care that we are perishing?"* (Mark 4:38). This was *their* wakeup call, not *His*, to properly perceive the perils of transition. The threatening storm without had no effect on Jesus because He didn't have one within. His supposed indifference to what they were going through was a misinterpretation of the entire experience. If we panic while in transition, we will always come to wrong conclusions about God's intentions. They didn't see the connection between what they had been taught earlier that day and what they were going through.

Sailing into the Wind

The wind is not always at your back as you transition. The old Irish blessing that says, "May the road rise up to meet you. May the wind always be at your back. May the sun shine warm upon your face, and rains fall soft upon your fields" sounds heartwarming, but it seldom works out that way during times of transition.

I think entrepreneur and motivational speaker Jim Rohn was right when he said, "The same winds blow on us all; the winds of disaster, opportunity and change. Therefore, it is not the blowing wind, but the setting of the sails that will determine our direction in life."

Transition often involves learning to sail into the wind. The physics of sailing are relatively easy as long as you happen to be going in the same direction the wind is blowing. The challenge is when the place you want to go also happens to be the direction from which the wind is blowing. This is when a maneuver called "tacking" comes into play. Ancient mariners learned very quickly that it was impossible to sail directly into the wind, or what is called the "no-go zone," because the sails did not catch enough wind to maintain forward momentum. Against intense headwinds, the boat's rudder is rendered completely ineffective in giving the boat direction. So, the mariners of old mastered a skill known as tacking. Instead of sailing directly into the wind, they would steer a zigzag course of at least forty-five degrees to either side of the direction from which the wind was blowing. They would steer their vessel making a run in one direction for a period of time, then they would then come about and sail a course forty-five degrees in the other direction. By sailing in this zigzag pattern, they would, by some mysterious interaction of ship, water, and wind, progress in a generally forward direction. They did not proceed directly to their goal but angled their way forward.

Bringing a boat about to angle in the opposite direction is one of the more tricky moves of sailing. When it is time to come about, the helmsman pushes the rudder hard to bring the boat around for a run at the other angle to the wind. As the boat comes about, it swings directly into the wind. For a few moments it loses its speed and momentum, the sails flap loose in the breeze, and everything seems out of control. In sailing lingo, this is known as "being in irons." As the bow continues to swing around and the wind fills the sails again, the large boom that controls the sail swings abruptly across the deck. Anyone looking in the wrong direction at this critical moment can end up with anything from a concussion to a cold dip in the ocean. As the sails fill with wind again, the boat heels over into another course and everybody on board must once again reorient themselves and reposition to balance the vessel. As dangerous and awkward as the whole process may be, tacking is the only way of getting from one point to another when you happen to be sailing into the wind.

There will always be plenty of people with negative *energy offering a problem for every solution. This usually comes from those who lack the courage to make the decisions that you need to make to move forward.*

A friend of mine told me that, as we navigate transition, there are three "tacking points" we are faced with: personal opinion, personal advantage, and personal convenience.

Personal opinions are the unsolicited armchair opinions that will rain down on you in the midst of transition. Giving in to personal opinion is acquiescing and abdicating to someone else's false narration of your life rather than navigating from your inner divine compass that points to true north. What you knew yesterday, and what others knew about you, could be irrelevant today. There will always be plenty of people with negative energy offering a problem for every solution. This usually comes from those who lack the courage to make the decisions that you need to make to move forward. "The greatest mistake you can make in life is to be continually fearing you will make one."[61]

Second, personal advantage may lower our risk tolerance and leave us unable to have enough adventure to discover the new possibilities that come with a transition. Consequently, what has previously been an advantage may become a disadvantage while in transition. Real advantages are more your about vantage point than anything else.

Then there is the issue of convenience. Am I opting to remain on the shores of personal convenience or am I willing to jettison what I believe to be essential cargo in order to find greater advantages that wait? Am I spending my life "waiting for my ship to come in" or am I aboard my own ship, tacking through changing winds?

Every Transition Involves Some Dying

A few years ago I came to a time of transition after having pastored for twenty-seven years. I had a large and thriving congregation that provided vocational and financial security for me. I was fulfilled in teaching the hungry hearts of my parishioners each week and in building community together. We envisioned growing old with familiar faces in one place well into our golden years.

We had started that church out with a congregation of only fifteen people, located in a rundown neighborhood that had been neglected and severely mismanaged for over sixty years. The church was drowning in debt and collection agencies were weekly threatening to sue. My wife was six months pregnant with our first child and I was in grad school when we moved into a parsonage that was structurally unsound and should have been condemned. Both the parsonage and the church building were in deplorable

61. "Daily Inspirations," *Psychology Tomorrow*, http://psychologytomorrowmagazine.com/the-greatest-mistake-you-can-make-in-life-is-to-be-continually-fearing-you-will-make-one-elbert-hubbard/ (accessed May 22, 2017).

condition. Most of the windows were broken, and it was surrounded by knee-high grass and various infestations. We didn't know then what we know now—that nothing we go through in life is wasted. Over time, by God's grace and our determination, which was empowered by His grace, we were able to retire the debt, sell the property, move to a new location, and begin to build. Long story short, within twenty years, our church was located on a fifty-acre campus of prime real estate with fifty thousand square feet of facilities, including a state-of-the-art sanctuary that held hundreds of people. We never forgot our beginnings, however, and we continued to reach back to impoverished neighborhoods in our area, as well as underwriting struggling churches.

So why, after rising from such a humble and ignominious beginning to success and status, would we ever entertain leaving? Many of my colleagues questioned my sanity. They were puzzled as to why I would even remotely consider leaving when I could have coasted through the second half of my life by staying put. I didn't know it at the time, but I was enrolling in a new curriculum. I would learn in the words of Carl Jung: "The first half of life is devoted to forming a healthy ego, the second half is going inward and letting go of it." Or as Jesus says to those that would follow Him,

> *Whoever wants to be my disciple must deny themselves and take up their cross and follow me. For whoever wants to save their life will lose it, but whoever loses their life for me will find it. What good will it be for someone to gain the whole world, yet forfeit their soul? Or what can anyone give in exchange for their soul?* (Matthew 16:24–26 NIV)

Worshipping Jesus is always easier than following Him, because merely worshipping Him involves no risk. Losing my life means I can find it? It sounds like an impossible sacrifice until you realize that my "life" for almost three decades had defined me in a certain way. Even my title of "reverend" or "pastor" was somewhat limiting. To lose that life was not really a loss but an invitation to a liminal space in order to experience more of who I would become. What I had been for twenty-seven years was not bad, but I had to let go of it. I had to essentially die to who I was to become who I would be. The "death" Jesus is speaking of is not just physical dying. It is a dying to what we have lived for or what we have done for a living.

In that sense, we all go through many deaths in our lifetime. The apostle Paul, who seemed to have nine lives, said, "*I die daily*" (1 Corinthians 15:31 KJV). Richard Rohr explains,

> All great spirituality teaches about letting go of what you don't need and who you are not. Then, when you can get little enough and naked enough and poor enough, you'll find that the little place where you really are is ironically more than enough and is all that you need. At that place, you will have nothing to prove to anybody and nothing to protect. That place is called freedom. It's the freedom of the children of God. Such people can connect with everybody. They don't feel the need to eliminate anybody.[62]

These deaths to the previous self are transitions and opportunities to experience transformation.

My exit strategy was rather tenuous due to never considering that I might do anything else but grow old doing what I had done for years. I had confidence in my competency and the relative security in my tenured position. For years I had found security in the sameness of pastoral responsibilities, and I was beginning to become complacent. Paradoxically, my competence in the job had bred a degree of complacency in me. I was too comfortable. If we don't regularly have something to overcome, we are susceptible to eventually being overcome by complacency. What we fear is

---

62. Richard Rohr, Thomas Keating, *Healing Our Violence through the Journey of Centering Prayer* (Cincinnati, OH: St. Anthony Messenger Press, 2010), audio recording.

actually quite ephemeral; something is unfamiliar to us, so it must be worse in some way, or so we think. Yet a quote attributed to Celestine Chua states, "Fear, uncertainty and discomfort are your compasses toward growth." Joseph Campbell wrote, "We must be willing to get rid of the life we've planned, so as to have the life that is waiting for us."[63]

If we don't regularly have something to overcome, we are susceptible to eventually being overcome by complacency.

Leaving the Comfort of the Nest

To say I was about to learn something about God and myself would be an understatement. I would be tutored in where my real security was and in extreme trust. Latent insecurities that I had been unknowingly carrying were about to surface. Until that time I knew what to expect from day to day for the most part. I was almost fifty years old and I began to learn that growth would demand the surrender of my perceived security. To evolve meant giving up familiar limiting patterns, relationships, and work that was risk-free but uninspiring. Maybe saying my work had become uninspiring is an overstatement. I had, without realizing it, taken my hands off the controls and switched to autopilot to some extent. Everything was too predictable. Turbulence was approaching that would require a firm grip for the next course correction.

I was beginning to experience something described in Deuteronomy as "the stirring of my nest." (See Deuteronomy 32:11.) The construction of an eagle's nest can take up to six weeks and it can be up to twelve feet in diameter and weigh two tons. The nest structure is made of limbs and is lined with animal skins to

63. Joseph Campbell, *Reflection on the Art of Living: A Joseph Campbell Companion*, Diane K. Osborn, ed. (New York: HarperCollins, 1991), 18.

create a soft and comfortable place for the eaglets to grow. Twelve weeks after hatching, the mother eagle swoops in one day and begins to stir or wreck the brooding area of the nest. She pulls out the soft leaves, tosses the rabbit fur to the winds, and removes the long vines that once provided comfort to them. The comfort during their early development is now a detriment.

Once the massive nest is gutted of its lining of comfort, it is now a skeleton of poking and provoking limbs. The mother eagle then begins to hover over the nest, violently flapping her massive wings creating turbulence that forces the young eagles out of the familiar and safe place. With the eaglets now forced out to the edge of the nest, they can now see the altitude of the loft where they have been incubated. The dizzying heights force them to summon the latent ability to leave the nest and experience flight for the first time. The mother eagle knows from her own memory of transition from eaglet to eagle that their reluctance is paralyzing. She will fly with aeronautic precision, scooping each one up on the tips of her wings and soaring up several thousand feet to allow them to feel the rush of flight. Then, without warning, she goes into a barrel roll maneuver like a fighter jet, sending them into a free fall. As the eaglets are hurtling from the tips of their mothers' wings toward terra firma, the instinct of flight awakens in them for the first time.

The imagery of an eagle violently stirring her nest and pushing her young eaglets out of their comfort zone into their destiny conveys the tumultuous nature of transitional discomfort. Like those eagles, God stirred my nest then and He continues to do so whenever I become too comfortable. In today's culture, it sounds counterintuitive, but comfort is overrated. Abraham Maslow said, "You will either step forward into growth or you will step backward into safety."[64] Learning to be comfortable with discomfort doesn't come naturally. It usually comes as a result of an unsolicited external force, provoking us out of our comfort zone and

---

64. As quoted in Brian Tracy, *How the Best Leaders Lead* (New York: Amacom Books, 2010), 35.

into the courage zone. To the unconscious mind, sameness equals safety and change equals danger. An internal shift has to occur for us to realize that comfort is not as comfortable as we thought and courage is not as dangerous as we thought. Our core beliefs have to be challenged for us to discover if they are true or not. God is forever unsettling the "settler" in all of us. I think it is true that we should face what we are afraid of and go live there.

To the unconscious mind, sameness equals safety and change equals danger. An internal shift has to occur for us to realize that comfort is not as comfortable as we thought and courage is not as dangerous as we thought. Our core beliefs have to be challenged for us to discover if they are true or not.

Maintaining focus during times of transition can be incredibly difficult. Our world is constantly bombarding us with attractions that distract us from what we should be focusing on. Take advertising for one example. Marketing experts have studied the human psyche and know how to break our focus throughout the day without us being aware of it. Who hasn't experienced the annoyance of their game on television being interrupted with loud, sometimes obnoxious, and cleverly-scripted commercials? The psychological "hooks" break our attention span with the fundamental rules of sales in mind: before they can sell us something, they first have to create a "sense of need," then a "sense of urgency." The product is presented as being something you must have, only there is a limited time and quantity available. It is designed to unsettle us, to distract us, to make us feel uneasy until we get to the store and buy their item. But once you get there, you might be distracted from what distracted you in the first place! There are "impulse" items strategically positioned in the checkout lines. You come into the store with one thing in mind and before you can get out of the door, you are distracted by something else. These examples may seem mundane, but they certainly remind us of the daily challenge of keeping the main thing, the main thing.

Taking Aim Takes Focus

Jesus said, *"No man having put his hand to the plough, and looking back, is fit for the kingdom of God"* (Luke 9:62 KJV). This statement is a word picture that illustrates the power of focus. To plow a field and maintain straight rows, a farmer sets his focus on something immovable, like a tree or a rock several yards away, and then he guides his plow toward it. If he takes his eyes off the object in the distance and looks down or around, the rows will not be straight. This was especially important in New Testament times because often the plot of land was limited in size. Rows that zig-zagged would hinder the growth and potential harvest.

A leftover from an agricultural society, "field" is the often-used term for our career or area of work. You may be in the field of education, finance, medicine, etc. And like an ancient farmer plowing his field, you too need focus to reap the fullest potential of your particular harvest.

I read a story many years ago about an Olympic marksman that further illustrates the power of focus. He was interviewed after winning the gold medal in this little-known Olympic event and was asked how he had developed his skills as a sharpshooter. To hit the bullseye of a target positioned hundreds of yards away with consistency is influenced by many factors: wind, velocity of the bullet, elevation changes from the shooter to the target, and the steadiness of the marksman's hands. To hone his skills, this shooter had physically conditioned himself to squeeze the trigger between heartbeats. He had learned how to control his respiration and the rhythm of his heart. Now that's focus!

David showed extreme focus, although still just a kid, when he took down Goliath. David was not distracted by the insults and threats of this mammoth of fear. He focused on the vulnerable opening in his enemy's seemingly invincible armor. Taking aim on the tiny opening in the giant's helmet, he hurled a smooth stone through the air with amazing accuracy, striking the brute in the forehead and toppling this mere distraction. David could have easily been diverted from his ultimate purpose by fixating on the incessant tirades of this formidable foe. The most powerful weapon used on these ancient battlefields was not a sword or spear but psychological domination. If your opponent can get inside your head, he has defeated you before the first blow has landed. David's future had already been secured by a sure prophecy, but the giant was sent to take his focus off of the future and onto an ostensible clear and present danger.

Like David, we have taunting giants that show up in our field of vision. Maybe you have heard the acronym for FEAR: *False Evidence Appearing Real*. We must remember that what lies within you and what awaits you are far greater than what is going on around you! Singleness of purpose is essential if you ever hope to navigate through the many transitions of life.

Jesus said, "*The light of the body is the eye: if therefore thine eye be single, thy whole body shall be full of light*" (Matthew 6:22 KJV). Obviously, we have two eyes, not just one, so what was implied by this statement? As with so many of the profound truths that fell from Jesus' lips, it has many applications. Visually, you are either right-eye dominant or left-eye dominant. In simple terms, this means that you prefer one eye to the other. You are able to focus with greater depth perception with either the right or the left eye. Avid hunters understand the importance of this if they are going to block out everything to the exclusion of their intended target. You may have never looked down the sight of a gun, but you have taken aim at objectives during your lifetime and cannot pull the trigger with confidence if you are not single-eyed.

Jesus was the epitome of someone who knew what to focus on and what to ignore; that is not to say that His life was not constantly cluttered with numerous distractions. He had voices demanding to be heard, victims vying for His virtue, and even well-intentioned friends and family members assuming He was ignoring things they deemed to be of great importance. The emotions of His mother came into play on a number of occasions. His brothers accused Him of losing His mind, and His beloved disciples were intimidated by His undaunted march toward the cross. But His resolve was unswerving. Once you make up your mind, you can't assume those around you will mind their own business. The second-guessers are always in opposition to the single-minded. Yet when concentrated with absolute intensity, the single-minded can cut like a laser beam through any objection or obstacle.

The second-guessers are always in opposition to the single-minded. Yet when concentrated with absolute intensity, the single-minded can cut like a laser beam through any objection or obstacle.

Jesus is described as "having a face set like a flint." (See Isaiah 50:7 NKJV.) Flint was an extremely dense stone used in ancient times for tools that needed to be able to withstand blow after blow without breaking. Jesus was not hardheaded but headed hard toward a singular purpose.

From the time we were children, we have been told to "pay attention" if we were going to learn valuable information. That phrase aptly describes the power of a single eye because it truly comes with a price. The eye's pupil is biologically programmed to regulate the amount of light that reaches the retina. When you step from bright sunlight into a dark room, the pupil opens wide to accommodate the lack of light. Light in Scripture is a metaphor for truth, and darkness is a metaphor for deception or ignorance. The world around us is growing more and more dark, but we can choose to position ourselves with a different perspective. Scripture says that God is the *"Father of lights, with whom is no variableness, neither shadow of turning"* (James 1:17 KJV). In Him there is no darkness or even a shadow. Surround yourself with images that flood your consciousness with faith, hope, and love.

You may think I have become a little extreme with this principle, but my wife and I have created a vision board that has Scriptures and pictures of all the things we are believing God for. I say this a lot, but it bears repeating: when we change the way we see things, the things we see will begin to change. Paul said it this way, *"We look not to the things that are seen* [or obvious] *but to the things that are unseen"* (2 Corinthians 4:18).

"Faith is the substance of things hoped for, the evidence of things not seen. For by it…we understand [how] *the worlds were framed"* (Hebrews 11:1–3 KJV). God framed the world by the image or picture He had of it. We have His nature, so we can create the frame for the picture He has of us by faith. When we focus on these things we have hope for, confident that the Lord brings nothing but light, and setting our face as a flint, we will be able to overcome transitions instead of letting them overcome us.

In Due Season

It has been said, "Healthy things grow; growing things change; change challenges us." In the information age, many mistakenly believe that information alone results in transformation. But transformation occurs when we successfully translate what is changing *within* us in relationship to what is changing *around* us.

The Greek philosopher Heraclitus said, "No man ever steps in the same river twice, for it's not the same river and he's not the same man." The only thing that is constant is change. I can hear some fundamentalist shouting, "God never changes!" I agree, at least partially. God's character never changes, but He is always changing His methods without notice.

It's like the change of literal seasons. A few months ago I felt something in the air that made me aware that change was on its way. I walked outside and did not feel the heavy and humid air that is so characteristic of our area in the summertime. Instead, I felt the crisp and cool air that is nature's announcement of fall's arrival. There is nothing quite like fall air; it is easier to breathe and it is invigorating to the senses in more than one way. Not only is the drop in temperature and the relief from months of oppressive humidity an indicator of change, but the foliage that has been emerald in color during the growing season of summer now begins to turn to different shades of mauve, red, and gold. Here in the southeastern part of the US, all through the Appalachians on up into the Northeast, the leaves will change in color as if God has taken His artist palette and, in a matter of days, splashed them with brilliant and breathtaking earth-tone colors.

The seasonal changes that come in His creation speak to us of the seasons in our own lives. It has always been my opinion that we live in far more manifestation than we realize. Romans 1:20 says, that *"the invisible things of* [God] *from the creation of the world are clearly seen"* (KJV). Ecclesiastes 3:1 says, *"To everything there is a season"* (KJV). We witness the coming and going of our seasons but seldom see that they reflect the seasons of our lives, and how God accomplishes His purposes. The colors of fall will last only a few short weeks before the leaves will drop off and leave the trees looking like gray skeletons silhouetted against the sky. In days to come, you will walk into the woods to the sound of leaves crunching under your feet. The leaves that had once created a canopy to the forest are now compost. As the winter rain, snow, and ice fall on them they will decay and in turn nourish the tree. What was alive in a previous season is now dying in order to give life next spring. The conundrum is that nothing lives without something dying.

Like the leaves changing in color and eventually letting go, we have to let go of the results of the last season. Though the majestic oaks, maples, and birch trees are now naked without their leaves, what has fallen to the ground will become a part of their root system. It is not just what we view above the ground that is important; it is the unseen roots that press their way through the soil downward and outward to support growth. The rich soil in which growth takes place is the result of countless seasons of falling leaves. Death gives way to life, which gives way to death, which gives way to life.

Yes, change is here for many. The change in the climate will necessitate you changing clothes. I know that's obvious. The shorts and the tank tops are put away and layers of clothing are put on. So embrace the changes; don't just change your wardrobe. Be clothed with a new attitude about the coming season. Breathe the fresh, crisp air of a new and unique time in your life. Let the roots of your identity in Christ go deeper than ever before. Change is in the air.

Wonderings

Exercises to Do While Wandering

Evaluate your tolerance for risk and change.
On a scale from 1 (intolerant) to 10 (very tolerant),
how tolerant are you to a change of:

Income: Would you take a financial risk to answer God's call?

Intolerant   Very Tolerant

1   2   3   4   5   6   7   8   9   10

Geography: Would you move somewhere else to answer God's call?

Intolerant   Very Tolerant

1   2   3   4   5   6   7   8   9   10

Vocation: Would you change jobs to answer God's call?

Intolerant   Very Tolerant

1   2   3   4   5   6   7   8   9   10

Education: Would you pursue more education to answer God's call?

Intolerant   Very Tolerant

1   2   3   4   5   6   7   8   9   10

If you circled anything lower than a "5," pray about that area of
intolerance and ask God whether or not it is blocking a call from
Him toward change.

List things you have done that involved opening yourself up to risk and change.

_____

_____

_____

_____

_____

_____

_____

List things you may consider pursuing that would involve risk or change.

_____

_____

_____

_____

_____

_____

_____

_____

REFLECTIONS

7

CONNECTING THE DOTS

Life is simply a connect-the-dots game,
and all the dots have already been identified and
organized by somebody else. All you have to do is
follow the blueprint, use their system, or work their
program to achieve similar results.[65]
—*Jack Canfield*

Do you remember the first time you saw a connect-the-dots picture? I do. I was probably five years old when I stumbled on it in the back of my coloring book. There, on the very last page, were numbered dots randomly sprinkled with no sequence. It seemed out of place since all the previous pages clearly depicted pictures with continuous lines. I was just beginning to develop the dexterity to color inside the lines when I was introduced to this new

---

65. Jack Canfield and Kent Healy, *The Success Principles for Teens* (Deerfield Beach, FL: Health Communications, Inc. 2008), 189.

challenge. I asked my mother what I was supposed to do with it. What she said seemed to have no rhyme or reason. Apparently, there was a picture encrypted that would emerge if I followed the numbers connecting each dot. At first it seemed senseless to erratically move my pencil across the page up and down from top to bottom and side to side until, about midway through, I began to see it. I didn't understand it then, but this was my primer to the process of connecting the dots in life that lead to purpose.

Serendipity

Years later, as an adult, I would read the words of the psalmist and gain understanding of what he wrote: *"the lines have fallen for me in pleasant places; indeed, I have a beautiful inheritance"* (Psalm 16:6). The *"lines"* probably allude to the division of the land by lot. The lots were measured off with roped lines. David knew that his spiritual land was in a beautiful place; he believed in an overruling destiny, which fixed the bounds of his purpose and his possessions.

In contemporary terms, if you own a home, you have a deed of trust with a plot plan that has a description of the metes and bounds of your property. At some point, a surveyor came to your property and measured its dimensions so you wouldn't trespass on your neighbor's property, or they on yours. The surveyor probably used a transit, which resembles a small telescope on a tripod. The surveyor looks through it at reference points (fence lines, trees, streams, or large rocks) to shoot the exact boundaries of your property.

Before we were born, God, the Sovereign Surveyor, looked through the telescope of time, sprinkling the dots of destiny over the map of our lives, predestining the people and the places in our lives. Earlier in the book, I referenced the often-used verse: *"And we know that for those who love God all things work together for good, for those who are called according to his purpose"* (Romans 8:28). The verse that follows speaks of predestination's relationship to purpose. *"And those whom he predestined he also called, and those whom he called he also justified, and those whom he justified he also glorified"* (verse 30).

Maybe you have heard of the concept of six degrees of separation. This proposed sociological phenomenon suggests that the world is smaller than we think. It claims that anyone on the planet is only removed from any other person on the planet through a chain of acquaintances that has no more than five intermediaries. I have experienced the so-called six degrees of separation phenomenon for years, way before you could "friend" someone across the world on Facebook or follow them on Twitter. The credibility of this idea has been in question ever since it was introduced in 1929. However, in today's world of Internet connectivity, it is more believable than ever.

We typically use the word *coincidence* to describe things that happen in our lives that are intriguing but seem to have no rhyme or reason. However, *coincidence* is also a word from geometry, the branch of mathematics concerned with shape, size, and the relative position of figures. I've found over the years, from uncanny experiences I've had, that my destiny or life path has been running parallel to that of others, and that, thanks to God's predestination, our parallel lines dip and bend in just the right place for us to converge at specific times and places. I have observed in each instance a complimenting of respective purposes.

The word *coincidence* appears only once in the New Testament, and it was used by Jesus in the parable of the Good Samaritan. In Luke 10:31, Jesus said, *"And by a coincidence a certain priest was going down in that way, and having seen him, he passed over on the opposite side"* (YLT). Our word *coincidence* is translated from the Greek word *synkyrian*, which is a compound of two words: *sun* and *kurios*. *Sun* means "together with," and *kurios* means "supreme in authority." So a biblical definition of *coincidence* could be "what occurs together by God's providential orchestration of circumstances."

God has seen fit to often remind me that what seem to be mere "coincidences" were actually convergence points. It is with some caution that I share with you the first time I noticed this pattern in my life's path and purpose and the way that God was nudging me with ever-so-subtle clues. I am cautious out of fear that some of you may think I am putting too much importance on what are only casual, happenstance occurrences—on coincidences. But I believe we must keep our eyes open for these things! As Richard Eyre writes in his book *Spiritual Serendipity,*

> The word *serendipity* was coined by the eighteenth-century British writer Horace Walpole, who defined it as "that quality of mind which, through awareness, sagacity, and good fortune, allows one to frequently discover something good while seeking something else." It is an attitude of mind and heart that attracts and enhances joy. As a mental approach, serendipity can energize your life by enabling you to balance spontaneity and structure and allowing you to harness time, not to manage it. As a spiritual quality, serendipity can create a bridge between your will and the will of the Divine, allowing your life to be guided and open to change.[66]

Serendipitous events, "coincidences," can be an incredible reassurance as we navigate new waters, overcomes challenges, or encounter transitions.

The Man from Jordan

The first time I noticed such serendipity was in 1987. I was leading a group of twenty-seven people on a tour of the Holy Land. We had flown from New York's JFK Airport, connected in Amsterdam, and then arrived in Amman, Jordan, late in the evening. We had dinner at the hotel and I was trying to get my

---

66. Linda Eyre and Richard Eyre, *Spiritual Serendipity* (New York: Simon & Schuster, 1997), cover.

jet-lagged traveling companions to bed since we had to get up very early the next morning to cross the Jordan/Israeli border and begin our week-long tour. It was around 11:00 p.m. when I closed my hotel room door for four quick hours of sleep. Minutes later there was a knock at door and I wondered who it could be. I had no idea that when I opened that door six thousand miles away from home, I was opening the door to an odyssey of connecting the dots.

Before me stood a representative of the tour company who had traveled with us. I knew immediately from the grim look on his face that something was seriously wrong. He looked at me and said, "Randall, we have just received news from the states that your wife has been in an automobile accident and we don't know the extent of her injuries." My mind immediately calculated the time difference as to what she may have been doing in her daily routine. I thought maybe the accident occurred around the time she would be picking up our two sons from daycare. In an instant I imagined a horrific crash and my entire family barely clinging to life. If this had happened today, I would have quickly been able to make contact with our family and assess the seriousness of the situation. But in 1987, no one had cell phones. I reached for the landline, calling the hotel operator who spoke broken English, and they connected me to an international operator equally inept at communicating in English.

For two hours, I bounced around, relaying my way by landline across the ocean until finally I reached the hospital room where my wife lay with a broken back. My father-in-law was with her and he assured me that she would be okay and that surgeons had said she would not experience any paralysis. She would be in a body brace and require complete bedrest for three months. I didn't question his truthfulness but I felt that he might not be telling me everything so as not to alarm me. I was sleep-deprived from the time difference and a grueling night of trying to confirm my wife's well-being. The sun was now coming up and I had to pull it together and assemble my tour group for the border crossing from Jordan into Israel. Of all the border crossings in the world at that time, this one was one of the most dangerous, given the tension between Israel and its easterly neighbor Jordan, but we crossed the border and cleared customs without incident.

For two days, I agonized over whether to return home or remain with the tour. The tour representative and the tour group understood my dilemma and assured me they would be fine with me returning. However, he informed me that there was one possible glitch. It was the Sabbath when I finally made my decision and the border was closed. My return tickets were in the Royal Jordanian Airlines office in Amman. It was not as simple as picking up the phone to leave a voicemail, or even faxing them to notify them that I was changing my ticket to return early. The only means of communication between these two countries was "telex," a network of teleprinters similar to a telephone network for the purposes of sending text-based messages—all of which are now obsolete! To make matters worse, messages had to travel from Jerusalem to Paris, then back to Amman. This was a primitive form of communication even back then. It would be like sending a message from New York to Boston via Miami.

Early in the morning after the Sabbath, I was waiting outside of the hotel in Jerusalem for a taxi to take me to the border that I had crossed forty-eight hours earlier. I had no confirmation that when I got to the airport in Amman, the airline would have received the telex concerning my ticket change and early return. The clock was ticking as I rushed into a taxi driven by an Arabic driver who drove wildly through the narrow streets of Old Jerusalem. We were only a few miles away from the hotel when he started talking on his radio. I understood nothing of what he said until I heard him say "Americano." I thought he might be talking about me but I wasn't sure. Then he did something that caused my heart to palpitate. He abruptly pulled over to the side of the road, jumped out of the taxi, and ran across the street. My mind was racing, thinking I would never make it to the border, through customs, and to the airport in time!

Soon, another driver came out of the building the first driver had entered. This new driver got in the car with me and off we went. This second driver said nothing as he erratically weaved in and out of traffic jams that included cars, pedestrians, and livestock. Finally we arrived at the border. I jumped out of the car and got in line at customs, all the while keeping watch on the time.

Fortunately, the customs process went without a hitch and finally I boarded the bus to cross the Allenby Bridge—the sole entry/exit point between Israel and Jordan. As soon as we reached the other side of the bridge, the bus stopped abruptly and two men got on calling out my name. I stood up from the back of the bus and they said I must go with them. I reluctantly responded to their request and exited the bus. They told me they were with the tour company and had come to expedite the process of getting me to the airport in time. I breathed a huge sigh of relief.

When I finally took my seat along with over four hundred other passengers on the 747 for the first leg of my trip home, I noticed a bag beneath the seat of the man in front of me with a tag that read "Charlotte, NC." That certainly arrested my attention since that was where I lived at the time. I attempted to communicate but discovered that he only spoke Arabic. It seemed a little odd to me that this man was traveling to the city where I lived.

I kept a close watch on the time during the hours of my transatlantic flight, keeping in mind the time difference. I had calculated that I would probably miss my domestic connection in New York for the final leg home. Sure enough, I missed my flight home and had to stay overnight in New York City. The next morning at the airport, I was not surprised to see the Jordanian gentleman on my rebooked flight home. Arriving in Charlotte, I forgot about the Jordanian man, retrieved my bags, and hurried to my house. My wife was home from the hospital and being cared for by family and friends. After getting up-to-speed on her prognosis, I went up the street from our house to buy groceries. Walking up and down the aisles of the grocery store, filling my cart, I saw him again. There in my hometown, in my neighborhood, was the man from the plane! What are the odds?

He didn't seem to notice me but I wanted to engage with him. Instead, however, I checked out, went to my car, and couldn't shake the urge to wait until he came out to follow him and see if he lived nearby. I tailed him and saw him turn into my subdivision and onto the street directly behind my house. Low and behold, a man from Amman, Jordan, six thousand miles away, sitting in front of me on my flight home, had moved to my neighborhood. A few weeks later, my wife and I were watching television when a public service announcement came on showing how our city was becoming an ethnic melting pot—and you guessed it—there he was on TV. Again, what are the odds?

Was this experience real or surreal? Was I exaggerating the importance of it? I could have been on another flight. I could have been sitting somewhere else on the plane of four hundred passengers and I would have never noticed the man who had moved practically into my backyard. I never saw the man again, so he wouldn't play a role in my destiny, however this cosmic coincidence made me conscious of the sort of divine connections that would come throughout the rest of my life. In the days and years that followed, I have received many upgrades in my understanding of how God speaks to us in ways that seem to be coincidental or even mundane. In the words of Andy Andrews,

> Little things do matter. Sometimes, little things matter the most. Everybody pays a lot of attention to big things, but nobody seems to understand that big things are almost always made up of little things. When you ignore little things, they often turn into big things that have become a lot harder to handle.[67]

---

67. Andy Andrews, *The Noticer Returns* (Nashville, TN: Thomas Nelson, 2013), 13.

Synchronicity

Just a few weeks ago I was connecting in the Atlanta International Airport—the busiest airport in the world, boasting one hundred million passengers per year. I had landed at one end of the airport, caught the train to the other side of the airport, and was waiting at my gate with a sea of people coming and going. As usual I was checking my phone for messages and social media. When I just happened to look up, walking by me was a dear friend from Australia. We were both astonished, knowing that this was just a reminder that no matter where we are on the dance floor of destiny, the Divine Choreographer knows our location and reminds us of our connection.

Again and again I have connected with people who have had a profound impact on my life through an uncanny and unusual series of events. This has heightened my understanding and awareness that our destinies were running parallel with one another and God had determined a time and place for our connection that could reveal our shared purpose. When we finally meet, the mutual feeling is "Where have you been all my life?" and "Why didn't we meet before now?" There is an immediate and mutual energy between us, causing us to realize that we have been looking for each other all our lives. Maybe, like me, you've found that some of these connections are even stronger than familial connections.

It really boils down to this: that all life is interrelated. We are all caught in an inescapable network of mutuality, tied together into a single garment of destiny. Whatever affects one directly, affects all indirectly.[68]

The interrelated nature of our lives is also known as *synchronicity*. Synchronicity is a concept originally coined by Carl Jung to describe meaningful coincidences as the "causal connecting principle" that links mind and matter and supersedes cause and effect.

---

68. Martin Luther King, *A Testament of Hope: The Essential Writings and Speeches of Martin Luther King, Jr.* (New York: HarperCollins, 1991), 254.

This has occurred many times in history, resulting in the simultaneous discoveries, and is well-documented in science.

Many in science view synchronicity as "apophenia," the experience of seeing false patterns in random or meaningless data. There is one caveat. An unhealthy obsession with synchronicity can create connections that are misleading. Not all synchronicities are meaningful! If we rely too much on synchronicity, it can take away our own free will and our ability to live intentionally, resulting in just passively waiting on "acts of God." Synchronicities, coincidences, divine connections—whatever you choose to call them—should not be made too much of, but certainly should not be made too little of, either.

Synchronicities, coincidences, divine connections—

whatever you choose to call them—

should not be made too much of,

but certainly should not be made too little of, either.

An often-misquoted Scripture is, "God works in mysterious ways, His wonders to perform." I say "misquoted" because it's not even from the Scripture at all; it's from a hymn by William Cowper and is not found in the Bible. But it alludes to this:

> *Oh, the depth of the riches and wisdom and knowledge of God! How unsearchable are his judgments and how inscrutable his ways! "For who has known the mind of the Lord, or who has been his counselor? Or who has given a gift to him that he might be repaid?" For from him and through him and to him are all things. To him be glory forever. Amen.*
>
> (Romans 11:33–36)

Throughout the Bible there are many instances of these divine connections between people, resulting in their respective destinies being fulfilled. For example, the servant of Abraham was sent out to search for a bride for Isaac. The servant traveled hundreds of miles who "just happened" to meet Rebecca, "the one," at a well. (See Genesis 24.) Joseph met two men in prison that "just happened" to be the butler and baker of Pharaoh. He interpreted their troubling dreams, which got him noticed by Pharaoh who had an equally troubling dream. It took years from the time Joseph, as a young man, had dreamed a dream of divine destiny for him to be separated by one degree of its fulfillment. (See Genesis 40.) Boaz noticed Ruth, who had been widowed and left destitute, as she gleaned for grain in a field and became his wife, strategically giving her a place in the messianic bloodline. *So she set out and went and gleaned in the field after the reapers, and she **happened** to come to the part of the field belonging to Boaz"* (Ruth 2:3).

Frederick Buechner's writings emphasize the importance of listening to your life. Buechner battles a fear of flying and describes that during one particularly anxious moment in an airport, he suddenly noticed on the counter a tiepin engraved with his initials—C. F. B. Another time, he was sitting on the side of the road one day during a dark time in his life. He noticed a car coming in his direction with a license plate that read T-R-U-S-T. Buechner believed, as I do, that there were messages in these chance occurrences of the underlying providence of God. These were moments of epiphany telling him to trust God, trust life—and to just trust.

Sometimes I'll think of a person I haven't seen or thought of for years, and ten minutes later I see him or her crossing the street. Or I turn on the radio to hear a voice reading the biblical story of Jael, which is the story that I have spent the morning writing about. Or a car passes me on the road, and its license plate consists of my wife's and my initials side by side.

When you tell people stories like that, their usual reaction is to laugh. I believe that people laugh at coincidence as a way of relegating it to the realm of the absurd and, therefore, of not having to take seriously the possibility that there is a lot more going on in our lives than we either know or care to know. Who can say what it is that's going on? But I suspect that part of it, anyway, is that every once and so often we hear a whisper from the wings that goes something like this: "You've turned up in the right place at the right time. You're doing fine. Don't ever think that you've been forgotten."[69]

Paying Attention

We all remember our elementary school teachers regularly telling us to "pay attention!" Usually that command would corral our focus for at least a few minutes before it had to be repeated again. Attention deficit disorder is a common condition today among many children. The symptoms, to mention just a few, include being easily distracted, missing details, forgetting things, having difficulty focusing on one task, and having difficulty processing information as quickly and accurately as others do. You may not have been diagnosed with this disorder, but when it comes to perceiving God's work in your life, it is very possible you could be suffering from it.

 Being aware is intentionally and consciously broadening the field of perception.
You are always conscious of the mind,
but you are not aware of yourself as being conscious.

Attention requires an intentionally focused awareness—an awareness of ourselves and of the people and patterns in our lives. What you need is to be aware of being aware. Being aware is intentionally and consciously broadening the field of perception. You

69. Frederick Buechner, *Beyond Words* (San Francisco: HarperSanFrancisco, 2004), 63.

are always conscious of the mind, but you are not aware of yourself as being conscious.

What exactly is the distinction here? Our minds produce thoughts continuously, even when we don't observe them. When you know what is going on in your mind, you call it "consciousness." Do you ever think about the way you think and wonder why you think that way? That is awareness! You begin to realize that you are not your thoughts when you can observe them.

The pace of our culture is constantly hurtling us into the future, and, as a result, we rarely experience the wholeness of the present. When I am speaking to an audience, I often realize that while their eyes may be open, they are not necessarily fully conscious—any more than their presence in the room means that they are fully there. Richard Rohr explains this succinctly:

> To become aware of God's presence in our lives, we have to accept what is often difficult, particularly for people in what appears to be a success-driven culture. We have to accept that human culture is in a mass hypnotic trance. We're sleep-walkers. All religious teachers have recognized that we human beings do not naturally see; we have to be taught how to see.[70]

Seeing God at work in the people and patterns in our lives is the act of recognition. Our journey develops symmetry when we can perceive Him at work in our everyday, ordinary lives. Unfortunately, in our modern world, the ordinary has been divorced from the supernatural. We have mistakenly bought into the belief that we have to somehow *rise up* to the supernatural, as if the supernatural is somewhere "up there" or "out there." The ordinary and the supernatural are not separate entities, as we have supposed, but rather, coexisting entities that reveal each other. God

---

70. Richard Rohr, *Everything Belongs* (New York: The Crossroad Publishing Company, 1999), 29.

reveals Himself through the actual, the here and now, or simply through *what actually is*. As Paula D'Arcy says, "God comes to us disguised as our life."

God speaks to us in many different ways and is always changing the medium. He speaks through those things that are hidden in plain sight more than we realize. *"For God does speak—now one way, now another—though no one perceives it"* (Job 33:14 NIV). Blindness has many forms. Maybe you've heard of color blindness, face blindness, blind spots, being blinded by love, or being too much in love. Have you heard of "change blindness"? Change blindness, simply put, is the failure to detect significant changes in your environment. It is the proverbial frog in the pot of boiling water. Our minds influence what we see, or don't see, more than we realize.

The ordinary and the supernatural are not separate entities,

as we have supposed, but rather,

coexisting entities that reveal each other.

Recognizing God in Our Everyday Moments

In His resurrected body, Jesus repeatedly appeared to His followers in several different forms. In most of these instances, it was difficult for them to recognize Him. I guess you could say that in these unexpected appearances, He looked like everybody else instead of appearing in shimmering celestial robes. Even before His resurrection, the disappointment felt by some was that Jesus was too earthy and didn't look significantly "spiritual" or "otherworldly" at all.

Consider the forms Jesus took during His resurrection appearances. Mary mistook Him for a gardener at the tomb.

But Mary stood weeping outside the tomb, and as she wept she stooped to look into the tomb. And she saw two angels in white, sitting where the body of Jesus had lain, one at the head and one at the feet. They said to her, "Woman, why are you weeping?" She said to them, "They have taken away my Lord, and I do not know where they have laid him." Having said this, she turned around and saw Jesus standing, but she did not know that it was Jesus. Jesus said to her, "Woman, why are you weeping? Whom are you seeking?" Supposing him to be the gardener, she said to him, "Sir, if you have carried him away, tell me where you have laid him, and I will take him away." Jesus said to her, "Mary." She turned and said to him in Aramaic, "Rabboni!" (which means Teacher).

(John 20:11–16)

Mary physically turns around and sees a man she supposes to be a gardener, but her awareness soon turns, as well.

Later, Jesus appeared to his forlorn disciples as a fisherman early one morning: *"Just as day was breaking, Jesus stood on the shore; yet the disciples did not know that it was Jesus. Jesus said to them, 'Children, do you have any fish?'"* (John 21:4–5). He was a carpenter and a rabbi in his earthly existence, but now he was a fisherman.

Jesus appeared as a stranger to two companions. They *"were going to a village named Emmaus, about seven miles out of Jerusalem, and they were talking with each other about all these things that had happened. While they were talking and discussing together, Jesus himself drew near and went with them. But their eyes were kept from recognizing him. And he said to them, 'What is this conversation that you are holding with each other as you walk?'"* (Luke 24:13–17).

They stood there, long-faced, as if they had lost their best friend—which they had. Then one of them, Cleopas, asked, *"Are you the only visitor to Jerusalem who does not know the things that have happened there in these days?"* (verse 18).

For seven miles they walked and talked with Jesus, and still they didn't recognize Him! How could they have not recognized Him? It seems He appeared out of thin air and joined their conversation. It seemed incredible to these men that He not heard the news about the crucifixion. It was not until hours later that their eyes were finally opened when He did something as ordinary as share a meal with them. We may expect or crave dramatic spiritual revelations, but in reality, the cosmic Christ is more intimate with us than we could ever imagine.

We may expect or crave dramatic spiritual revelations,

but in reality, the cosmic Christ is more intimate

with us than we could ever imagine.

Frederick Buechner wrote, "The sacred moments, the moments of miracle, are often the everyday moments, the moments which, if we do not look with more than our eyes or listen with more than our ears, reveal only…the gardener, a stranger coming down the road behind us, a meal like any other meal. But if we look with our hearts, if we listen with our whole being and our imagination… what we may see is Jesus himself."[71]

As the poet Mary Oliver says, "Ten times a day something happens to me like this—some strengthening throb of amazement—some good sweet empathic ping and swell. This is the first, the wildest and the wisest thing I know: that the soul exists and is built entirely out of attentiveness."[72] It has been said that what we focus on determines what we miss.

71. Frederick Buechner, *The Magnificent Defeat* (New York: HarperCollins, 1966), 87–88.
72. Quoted in Angeline Haen, *Sweet Wisdoms* (Brunswick, Maine: Shanti Arts Publishing, 2017), front matter.

"Nature is built on an infinite number of coincidences, and their presence in your life will soon become apparent."[73] Pay attention. Take notice of the coincidences that occur in your life. Write them down and see if a pattern doesn't begin to develop. Awareness, or consciousness, is essential to connecting the dots of your destiny. Through awareness and intention we begin to see the relationship between phenomena in our lives that are worthy of our attention that ultimately lead to enlightenment and growth.

73. Deepak Chopra, M. D., "SynchroDestiny," https://www.scribd.com/doc/73651243/SynchroDestiny-Deepak-Chopra-Free-PDF-Library-1 (accessed May 22, 2017).

Wonderings

Exercises to Do While Wandering

List some "coincidences" that have changed or impacted your life in some way. It may have been being in the right place at the right time, a random connection with a person of importance or influence, an opportunity that landed in your lap in a way you cannot explain, etc.

_____

_____

_____

_____

_____

_____

_____

_____

_____

_____

_____

_____

What might God be telling you from these occurrences?

_____

_____

_____

_____

_____

_____

_____

If there is more than one, can you see any pattern between them?

_____

_____

_____

_____

_____

_____

_____

_____

REFLECTIONS

EPILOGUE:
WHAT A DIFFERENCE A DAY MAKES

Congratulations if you have made it this far. Good things can be found down the road if we don't stop walking, keeping in mind that life is about enduring difficult, enigmatic days in order to arrive at the best days. Believe it or not, everything is within walking distance if we have the time and perspective. Perspective really is everything, or as Thoreau put it: "It's not what you look at that matters, it's what you see."

Hopefully, by now, you've gained a greater appreciation and perspective for the sometimes lengthy but always ongoing process that leads to purpose in life.

What a difference one day can make to that purpose!

The 1993 film *Groundhog Day*, starring Bill Murray and Andie MacDowell, illustrates this point. Murray plays Phil Connors, a self-absorbed TV weatherman who is sent on a dreaded assignment to Punxsutawney, Pennsylvania, to cover the annual emergence of the groundhog, foretelling whether there will be an early spring or six more weeks of winter. Through some mystical occurrence of movie magic, Murray becomes trapped in a surreal time loop in which he repeats the same day over and over until he slowly grows in character and, in the process, discovers his ultimate purpose. The inane repetition he is caught in is a clear metaphor for a typical life. The film's popularity is testament to the fact that most people can relate very well to Phil's quandary of feeling trapped in a mundane, superficial, and even meaningless existence.

At first, Phil deals with his boredom and angst in hedonistic ways, but eventually he entertains suicidal thoughts. After finally choosing to make use of the seemingly endless time he has been given by embracing change, he wakes up to discover that February 3 has indeed arrived and his ordeal is over. He has escaped the time-loop prison. It's unclear how much time elapsed. Possibly weeks, months, maybe even years.

Harold Ramis and Danny Rubin co-wrote the movie. In an interview, Rubin said, "The movie shows that it is the repetition of days itself which pushes us forward in our own maturation as we start to encounter the same things over and over again." Rubin continued, "The very first time he's presented with [the repeating day], it's probably the worst day of his life. And, by the end of the movie, we see that it's the exact same day but somehow this is probably the best day of his life."[74]

The Scriptures are replete with examples of dire situations turning around in a day. There is a verse that has been referenced so many times, I am hesitant to mention it. It has been worn smooth with familiarity: *"This is the day that the LORD has made; let us rejoice and be glad in it"* (Psalm 118:24). I think many have glibly parroted this verse and been disappointed, thinking that it

---

74. Ted Slowik, "Slowik: Here's why 'Groundhog Day' is the greatest movie ever made," *Chicago Tribune*, January 31, 2017, http://www.chicagotribune. com/suburbs/daily-southtown/opinion/ct-sta-slowik-groundhog-day-st-0201-20170131-story.html (accessed June 7, 2017).

was some scriptural incantation, like *abracadabra*. However, the verse isn't effectual until you realize it is a declaration followed by a decision.

On most days you probably concede that one day seems no different than the rest. Everywhere you look there are reminders. Your morning looks the same, your commute looks the same, and your job looks the same. Your bank account is unchanged and your financial debt remains. Bills arrive in the mail, the demands of life call out to you, and on and on it goes.

I am convinced that what makes the difference is when we decide to declare this is not just another day, but a day that God has uniquely made! When we begin to live each day in expectancy rather than dread, things will indeed begin to change. Dread abdicates each day to all those things that seem unalterable and inevitable. It is the "Que Sera, Sera" attitude of "whatever will be, will be."

God does not respond to dread but to declarations that acknowledge His sovereignty. Destiny comes to those who make God-inspired decisions that defy the odds. There are really only two options, no matter what our circumstances are: dread the day or declare the day as His. You can go to bed one night sick, in debt, or distressed and wake up the next morning to the difference a new day makes.

There are days in which your process may seem more like nomadic drifting, but if you trust it, God will use these days to lead you from wandering to purpose, from a state of wondering what difference your life makes to a supernatural destination culminating in the realization of your destiny. Don't give up and lose patience. Don't waste each new day you are given. They all accumulate in the reservoir of your edification. They are all necessary steps in taking you from where you are to where you were meant to be. Truly, this *is* the day the Lord has made. Let us rejoice and be glad *in* it!

Bon voyage.

ABOUT THE AUTHOR

Randall Worley pastored a thriving congregation for twenty-five years. For the last nine years, he has traveled around the world, providing apostolic consultation to church leadership and teaching in churches and conferences on kingdom issues by providing ground-breaking revelation. Randall received his PhD in religious philosophy in 2009. His cutting-edge articles have been published in many leading Christian publications. He is a regular guest instructor in some of the nation's leading schools of ministry, preparing believers to impact the world with kingdom influence. As a life coach, Dr. Worley has worked with individuals in the business community desiring to integrate kingdom principles into the marketplace. In 2015, he self-published *Brush Strokes of Grace*. Randall and his wife, Penny, have three adult sons who are all uniquely involved in various aspects of lifestyle ministry.

RandallWorley.com

REFLECTIONS

_____
_____
_____
_____
_____
_____
_____
_____
_____
_____
_____
_____
_____
_____
_____
_____
_____
_____
_____
_____
_____

REFLECTIONS

Welcome to Our House!

We Have a Special Gift for You

It is our privilege and pleasure to share in your love of Christian books. We are committed to bringing you authors and books that feed, challenge, and enrich your faith.

To show our appreciation, we invite you to sign up to receive a specially selected **Reader Appreciation Gift**, with our compliments. Just go to the Web address at the bottom of this page.

God bless you as you seek a deeper walk with Him!

WE HAVE A GIFT FOR YOU. VISIT:

whpub.me/nonfictionthx

Whitaker House